esp

EXTRASENSORY
PERCEPTION

By

SIMEON EDMUNDS

1973 EDITION

Published by

W ILSHIRE BOOK COMPANY
12015 Sherman Road
No. Hollywood, California 91605
Telephone: (213) 875-1711

© 1965, by Aquarian Press • PUBLISHER
Library of Congress Catalog Card Number: 65-12377

Printed by
HAL LEIGHTON PRINTING CO.
P. O. Box 1231
Beverly Hills, California 90213
Telephone: (213) 346-8500

Printed in the United States of America
E-10

INTRODUCTION

A WITCH-DOCTOR works his ju-ju, and hundreds of miles away his victim, all unaware of the magic being performed against him, falls sick, weakens, and within a few days is dead—in a manner and from a cause for which modern medical science is unable to offer even the glimmer of an explanation, much less provide any prophylactic or antidote.

A patient suffering from an "incurable" condition, congenital ichthyosis, a hideous scaling of the skin, recovers to a fantastic degree as the result of a hypnotist's suggestions.

A fortune-teller predicts, accurately and with a wealth of detail, the manner in which a young man will meet his death many years later.

The alleged spirit of a dead man gives information, subsequently verified, concerning facts of which no living person, by any normal process, could have been aware.

A group of sober, respected men, of unquestioned integrity, assert that in their presence a man floated through the air, out of a fourth floor window and in through that of an adjoining room.

An experimental subject determines, purely by the exercise of will, the face that will be uppermost when a die falls.

An apparition, which she identifies as that of her dead husband, warns a widow of impending danger.

Miracles? Traveller's tales? Far-fetched fiction? — Or sober facts? The credulous and uncritical, of course, hail these things as evidence for the "supernatural," while the hard-headed sceptic, with little more reason and rather less excuse, dismisses them all as superstitious nonsense. To the open-minded, who will neither accept blindly nor make sweeping dismissals, the answer is not so simple. The examples I have given, for instance, are not extracts from the fables of a less critical age, nor are they the bizarre creations of imaginative novelists. They are taken from a vast literature of scholarly reports of serious scientific investigation and experimentation carried out during the past hundred years into what is usually termed the supernormal, paranormal, or psychical.

This book has not been written for the advanced student of parapsychology, nor, on the other hand, is it a special attempt to proselytize or to convince the sceptic. Its purpose is to make information, much of it already on record but widely distributed throughout an extensive and somewhat technical literature, more accessible for the newcomer to this fascinating field of enquiry, and to give an outline of the history, scope and present-day position of parapsychology, together with a comment on some current theories and speculations concerning its future.

ACKNOWLEDGMENTS

THANKS for permission to quote are gratefully extended to the following:

Miss Lucille Iremonger, author of *The Ghosts of Versailles,* and her publishers, Messrs. Faber and Faber, London.

The Council of the Society for Psychical Research and the editor of its *Journal and Proceedings,* Mr. G. W. Fisk.

Dr. Milan Rýzl.

Mr. W. H. Salter.

Dr. D. J. West.

The author is also indebted to Mr. Martin Ebon, editor of the *International Journal of Parapsychology,* and Mr. F. Clive-Ross, editor of *Tomorrow* magazine, for permission to use extracts from his own articles which have appeared in those journals.

Sources of illustrations are acknowledged individually.

S.E.

CONTENTS

ILLUSTRATIONS

Also by Simeon Edmunds:
Hypnotism and the Supernormal
Aquarian Press, London, 1961.

Chapter 1

THE FIELD OF ENQUIRY

> *"Observations culled from many sources lead us to believe*
> *that there are forces existing in nature which are still*
> *unmeasured and undefined, awaiting provable hypotheses*
> *and explanations. One great adventure available to us is*
> *to examine, as far as we possibly can, those indications that*
> *appear to imply the existence of an invisible but nevertheless*
> *intelligent source in the universe within and around us."*
>
> EILEEN J. GARRETT

THROUGHOUT the history of the human race, from the simplest
primitive tribes to the greatest civilized nations, there has existed
a belief in what is commonly called the *supernatural*: the occurrence of strange phenomena in apparent defiance of natural laws.
Many manifestations once thought miraculous—comets and eclipses,
for example—have been shown by advancing science to be normal
parts of the order of nature, and are now thus regarded even if
incompletely understood. Reports of other phenomena have, however, persisted throughout history. Whatever their source, in both
time and location, these reports all bear a remarkable similarity,
covering such alleged happenings as hauntings and apparitions,
"second sight," miraculous healing of the sick, "thought transference," prevision, communications from the dead and other events
associated with the seance-room, etc. Many of these reports are
seemingly by men of probity and judgement, and colored though
they undoubtedly are by the environment and beliefs of those who
made them, bear witness to the occurrence of phenomena that
appear to defy natural laws.

Although it is a reasonable *prima facie* assumption that there
might well be a factual basis to some of these accounts at least, it
was not until the advent in the nineteenth century of the "age of
honest doubt" that any serious investigation of these phenomena
was attempted. Even then, only a small, enlightened minority
deemed these claims worthy of examination, most scientists of the

3

day disdaining to consider anything that did not appear to conform
with their own tidy mechanistic theories, and it is not surprising
that scientific investigation into the *supernormal* or *paranormal,*
as the subject became known, was at first the lonely task of a few
courageous, uncoordinated pioneers.

Interest in the subject was stimulated during the early part
of the last century, first by the claims of some of the early "magnetizers" and "mesmerists" that certain of their entranced subjects
exhibited supernormal powers, and soon afterwards by the rapid
growth of the cult of spiritualism and the even more fantastic claims
of its "mediums" and their disciples. As a consequence, a number
of scholars and scientists, including several of the most eminent
savants of the period, turned to the exploration of what one of
them, Sir William (then Professor) Barrett, described as "that
debatable borderland between the territory already conquered by
science and the dark realms of superstition and ignorance."[1] The
alleged phenomena investigated became known as *psychic,* and the
new field of enquiry was termed *psychical research,* by which desig-
nation it is still widely recognized. In recent years, however, the
name *parapsychology* has become increasingly employed and is
considered by many to be more in keeping with current experimental methods and theories. Some workers draw a distinction
between the two terms, using "psychical research" as a generic
name for all work in this field, confining "parapsychology" to
purely experimental work as distinct, for instance, from the investigation of spontaneous phenomena and the claimed experiences
of others. Throughout this book, in conformity with the most
common practice, the two terms are regarded as synonymous.

The word "parapsychology" possesses one important advantage over "psychical research," however. The latter has long been
regarded by disinterested laymen, and indeed by many of the less
knowledgeable of the spiritualists, as a synonym for "spiritualism,"
a completely erroneous identification which cannot be too strongly
and too frequently refuted. For this reason alone, the employment
of a term which does not have such unfortunate associations is most
desirable. The claims of spiritualism will be considered later at
some length, but at this stage it may be well to stress that although

the so-called spiritualistic phenomena are·a proper and important object of enquiry for the parapsychologist, their study—or for that matter, their possible acceptance as factual—does not by any means imply the acceptance of "spiritualistic" explanations of them.

It will be easier to make clear the scope, aims and achievements of modern parapsychology through a brief historical survey, explaining various points and giving the meanings of specialized terms as they arise. I will try to avoid esoteric expressions and technical jargon whenever more everyday language will suffice.

As we have noted, serious scientific interest in the paranormal was aroused largely by the repeated claims of the early mesmerists that certain gifted subjects were able, when in trance, to demonstrate the possession of extraordinary psychic faculties. These faculties included the ability to read the thoughts of others, to act upon the "willed" but unspoken commands of the mesmerist, and to see and report on events occurring in distant places, the first two of these being examples of what was later to be designated *telepathy*, and the last a form of *clairvoyance*. Mesmer (1733-1815) made similar claims, also asserting that "at times the somnambule [deeply entranced subject] can perceive the past and the future by means of the inner sense." We shall see later that many eminent men claimed to have observed such things and bore testimony to their truth.

The mesmeric, or hypnotic, trance forms a convenient link with the second subject to which parapsychology owes its origin, namely spiritualism, for the "trance" of the "medium," in which alleged communications from and sometimes control of the medium by the spirits of the dead takes place, is undoubtedly a form of hypnosis, usually self-induced.

Other forms of "spiritualistic" phenomena demanding investigation included the levitation of heavy objects, the production of "spirit" writings on slates and in sealed packets, spirit voices, materialization of spirit forms, "psychic" photography, table turning and the like. The phenomena just listed come in the category of "physical" phenomena, as distinct from the "mental" kind such as trance speaking, "clairvoyantly" perceived descriptions of and messages from (it is claimed) the dead, automatic writing, etc.

Although similar beliefs have existed among many races and in many different periods of history, and although their roots are readily traceable back through mesmerism and "animal magnetism," religious cults such as the "Shakers," and the Swedish seer, Swedenborg, spiritualism as we know it began in 1847, when Andrew Jackson Davis, of Poughkeepsie, New York, known variously as the "Poughkeepsie Seer" and the "Prophet of the New Revelation," published a book entitled *The Principles of Nature, Her Divine Revelations.* Davis, who was a somnambule claiming to be in touch with the spirits of many illustrious dead, including Galen and Swedenborg, made a number of extraordinary prophesies in his book, stating it was true that spirits commune with one another when "one is in the body and the other on higher spheres" and predicting that the truth of his claim would soon be demonstrated.

The following year, in Hydesville, New York, the first of the famous "Hydesville knockings" was reported. The home of the Fox family, where they took place, was a tiny wooden cottage, so small that John D. Fox, his wife and two daughters, Margaretta, aged fifteen, and Katie, aged twelve, all shared the same bedroom. One night in March, 1848, when the girls were lying in their bed, a series of loud raps was heard, seemingly produced by some intelligence which, once a code had been established, was able to answer questions. It claimed to be the spirit of a peddler who had been murdered and buried in the cellar. The story spread rapidly, and a married sister of the girls, finding that she too could cause raps to be produced, teamed up with them on a commercial basis. In 1851 a team of investigators from Buffalo University examined the sisters and, it would seem, showed them to be fraudulent, concluding that the raps were produced by the girls snapping the joints of their toes and knees. A relation by marriage then made a sworn statement that the girls had told her the whole thing was a fake, and demonstrated how the raps were made. By this time, however, numerous other rapping "mediums" had set up in competition with the Fox sisters. Thirty-eight years later the sisters made public confessions of fraud, and Margaretta toured the country demonstrating how she "rapped" by cracking her toe joints. The confessions were subsequently recanted, presumably as the sisters hoped to go back into the "business," but the confessions and demonstrations are too well authenticated for us to be in any doubt about them. These admissions had little effect on the growth of spiritualism, which had spread throughout the Western world, with a host of "mediums" producing not only raps but the whole range of phenomena listed on pages 66-70 and much more besides.

Most of these "mediums" were, without doubt, fraudulent, and many were caught and exposed; but there were some who submitted to investigation, were never detected in any form of trickery, and who, on the face of it, seem to have produced genuine phenomena. This fact has been advanced as one of the reasons why the confessions of the Fox sisters and other charlatans of their day did but little damage to the growth of the new "movement." Outstanding among these apparently genuine mediums was Daniel Dunglas Home (1833-86), the most famous of all "physical" mediums and practically the only well known one of this kind against whom no charge of fraud was ever substantiated. His mediumship will be discussed at some length in a later chapter.

Home was investigated by the famous scientist Sir William (then Professor) Crookes; and several other leading scientists of the day, including Professors William Barrett, Ray Lancaster and Alfred Russel Wallace, made researches into the claims of other prominent mediums, several of whom were exposed. The first attempt at organized investigations was made in 1851 with the founding of a "Ghost Society" at Cambridge, and in 1869, the London Dialectical Society, a body whose purpose was "affording a hearing to subjects which are ostracized elsewhere, especially those of a metaphysical, religious, social or political character," appointed a committee "to investigate the phenomena alleged to be Spiritual Manifestations, and to report thereon." This committee, after interviewing witnesses, reading statements and attempting some minor experiments, at length issued a report accepting the genuineness of a variety of phenomena and concluding that "the subject is worthy of more serious attention and careful investigation than it has hitherto received."[2]

The evidential standards of this committee were deplorably low, many phenomena of a patently fraudulent nature being accepted on the words of a few credulous witnesses, and it is hardly surprising that *The Times* described the report as "nothing more than a farrago of impotent conclusions, garnished by a mass of the most monstrous rubbish it has ever been our misfortune to sit in judgement upon." Although such scathing comment was in fact all that the report merited, it did prove of service by focussing the attention of a number of more critical investigators on the subject. Another useful purpose served by the report has been pointed out by Podmore, one of the most critical of the early researchers. He says:

"The work done by the Dialectical Society was, no doubt, of value, since it brought together and preserved for us a large number of records of personal experience by representative spiritualists. For those who wish to ascertain what spiritualists believed at this time, and what phenomena were alleged to occur, the book may be of service. But, except in the minority report by Dr. Edmunds, there is no trace of any critical handling of the material, and the conclusions of the committee can carry little weight."[3]

In 1875, several prominent researchers formed a "Psychological Society" for the investigation of alleged supernormal phenomena, but this was dissolved four years later on the death of one of its leading members.

In 1882, William Barrett, who had been carrying out experiments in hypnosis and "thought-transference," consulted several other workers, with a view to founding a permanent, properly constituted society. In his own words:

"A new and promising field of scientific enquiry was thus opened up, and it was necessary that other investigators should either verify or disprove the evidence so far obtained on behalf of a faculty hitherto unrecognized by science. But such an investigation lay outside the scope of any existing scientific society; it therefore seemed essential to form a new Society to carry on the inquiry and publish the results obtained. Accordingly, after consultation with Mr. Myers, Mr. Romanes and others, a conference was called by the present writer, at which an account was given of the evidence so far obtained on behalf of thought-transference and other psychic phenomena. This resulted in the foundation of the Society for

Psychical Research in January 1882, an investigation of the evidence on behalf of thought-transference being the first work undertaken by the Society."[4]

An official statement issued later by the Society (hereinafter referred to as the SPR), giving the reasons for its inception, typifies the restrained and cautious attitude which it has always adopted and still maintains:

"The Society for Psychical Research, which was incorporated in August, 1895, was founded at the beginning of 1882, for the purpose of making an organized and systematic attempt to investigate various sorts of debatable phenomena which are *prima facie* inexplicable on any generally recognized hypothesis. From the recorded testimony of many competent witnesses, past and present, including observations recently made by scientific men of eminence in various countries, there appeared to be, amidst much illusion and deception, an important body of facts to which this description could apply, and which, therefore, if incontestably established, would be of the very highest interest. The task of examining such residual phenomena has often been undertaken by individual effort, but never hitherto by a scientific society organized on a sufficiently broad basis."

The principal divisions of the Society's work were set out thus:

1. An examination of the nature and extent of any influence which may be exerted by one mind upon another, otherwise than through the recognized sensory channels.

2. The study of hypnosis and mesmerism, and an inquiry into the alleged phenomena of clairvoyance.

3. A careful investigation of any reports, resting on testimony sufficiently strong and not too remote, of apparitions coinciding with some external event (as for instance a death) or giving information previously unknown to the percipient, or being seen by two or more persons independently of each other.

4. An enquiry into various alleged phenomena apparently inexplicable by known laws of nature, and commonly referred by spiritualists to the agency of extra-human intelligence.

5. The collection and collation of existing materials bearing on the history of these subjects.

The stated aim of the Society was "to approach these various problems without prejudice or prepossession of any kind, and in the same spirit of exact and unimpassioned inquiry which has enabled science to resolve so many problems, once not less obscure nor less hotly debated."

The SPR followed this program so successfully that any history of early parapsychology must inevitably be predominantly a history of that society, for not only was by far the greatest amount of serious early research carried out under its auspices, but its *Journal* and *Proceedings,* which have been published continuously since it was founded, probably contain more detailed information and carefully compiled reports than the whole of the remaining literature of psychical research put together.

An important Note, which appeared in the original Constitution of the SPR and still applies, reads: "To prevent misconception, it is here expressly stated that Membership of the Society does not imply the acceptance of any particular explanation of the phenomena investigated, nor any belief as to the operation, in the physical world, of forces other than those recognized by Physical Science." The founder members were by way of being a "mixed bag," and included scientists, classical scholars and philosophers, doctors, clergymen and politicians. Some were convinced spiritualists, others highly sceptical. By far the most influential section was that known as the "Cambridge group," led by two of the most distinguished of all psychical researchers, Edmund Gurney and Frederic W. H. Myers. Both classical scholars of distinction, they were only persuaded to join the new society on the undertaking to become President by another Cambridge man, Professor Henry Sidgwick, whom they knew to be keenly interested in the subject. William Crookes and Alfred Russel Wallace became members soon afterwards. Throughout its history the SPR has numbered many eminent men among its members and on its Council, and many illustrious names have honored its Presidential Chair.

The first major work carried out under the auspices of the SPR was the compilation, mainly by Myers, Gurney and Podmore, of *Phantasms of the Living,* begun in 1883 and published in 1886. One of the great standard works of parapsychology, it deals, to quote the authors, with "all classes of cases where there is reason to suppose that the mind of one human being had affected the mind of another without speech uttered, or word written or sign made—had affected it, that is to say, by other means than through the recognized channels of sense." It is concerned largely with the consideration of the standards of evidence necessary in psychical research, particularly when assessing the value of reports of spontaneous phenomena, and stresses the defects to which such reports are particularly subject. It also deals at length with various aspects of hallucinations and the different psychological conditions conducive to their production. These discussions are based largely on experimental work by the authors, and also on the reports of a great number of spontaneous cases, some of earlier origin and others collected for the purpose.

In 1885, the SPR, impressed by accounts of the feats of Madame Blavatsky, the founder of the Theosophical Society, sent Dr. Richard Hodgson, a competent and critical investigator, to India for first hand reports. Hodgson established that far from being miraculous, Madame Blatvatsky's phenomena, including the famous "Koot Hoomi" letters which purported to have come from the Mahatma in a miraculous manner, were completely fraudulent. These letters Hodgson proved to be in Madame Blavatsky's own handwriting, and he interviewed one of her confederates who wrote a full confession of her part in the deceptions. The SPR report on Madame Blavatsky concludes: "We regard her neither as the mouthpiece of hidden seers nor as a mere vulgar adventuress; we think she has achieved a title to permanent remembrance as one of the most accomplished, ingenious, and interesting impostors in history."

In 1885, largely as the result of a lecture tour in the previous year by Sir William Barrett, an American Society for Psychical Research was formed, with headquarters in Boston (not to be confused with the American Psychical Society, which was founded in Boston in 1892 and, after publishing seven quarterly issues of *The Psychical Review,* closed down in 1895). After two years Richard Hodgson went to America and became secretary of the ASPR, which soon afterwards became affiliated as a branch of the British Society, remaining thus until Hodgson's death in 1905, when it again be-

came an independent body, this time under the direction of a celebrated American researcher, Professor James Hyslop.

The SPR suffered a great loss by the death, in 1888, of Edmund
Gurney, who, in addition to his part in the production of *Phantasms
of the Living,* had carried out notable work in the field of hypnotism. He was, according to Myers, "the first Englishman who
studied with any kind of adequate skill the psychological side of
hypnotism." Dr. T. W. Mitchell, a prominent member of the SPR
and himself no mean authority on hypnotism, wrote later that
Gurney's experimental findings "were received with incredulity,
and few realized that he was laying the foundations on which the
psychology of abnormal mental states during the next twenty
years was to be based."

At the time of his death, Gurney was compiling a census of
persons who, in answer to a questionnaire, had claimed to have
seen an apparition or a vision which they recognized; and this
work, still far from completion, was taken over by a committee
under Professor Sidgwick and enlarged in scope. Over 17,000
answers were examined, and of these more than 2,000 were from
persons who claimed to have seen an apparition. The report, known
as the "Census of Hallucinations,"[5] was published in 1894.

In 1900, the SPR received another serious blow through the
death of its President, Henry Sidgwick, and less than a year later
an even greater one when Myers died also. Their deaths, and the
turn of the century, marked the close of an epoch in parapsychology,
and the end, in some respects, of a "golden age," in psychical research.

Much of the most important work of this era, however, was
embodied in books not published till the next decade.

The year 1902 saw the publication of one of the greatest of
all classics of psychical research: Frank Podmore's *Modern Spiritualism*. Podmore had once been an ardent spiritualist and a
frequent contributor to journals supporting the subject. The exposure of several mediums in whom he had formerly believed,
however, changed his outlook to one of extreme scepticism, and
this attitude he maintained until within a short time of his death.
In *Modern Spiritualism,* Podmore traces, with great erudition and

THE FIELD OF ENQUIRY

13

skill, the evolution of spiritualism from its remotest beginnings, and although it has been argued, and with some reason, that his cynicism sometimes sullies his impartiality, few would seriously contend that any other history of spiritualism—and there are many —can remotely approach it in accuracy, detail, objectivity and literary quality. Of almost equal importance and comparable quality is another of Podmore's books which became a standard work, *Mesmerism and Christian Science,* published in 1909, a year before his death.

Modern Spiritualism became, on publication, by far the most important and comprehensive work in the literature of psychical research, but it was destined to retain this position for only a few months. In February, 1903, came the publication of the monumental *Human Personality and Its Survival of Bodily Death,* the culmination of Myers's life-work, which was nearing completion at the time of his death. It was completed and prepared for publication, at Myers's express wish, by Richard Hodgson and another well-known researcher of the time, Alice Johnson. In it Myers coordinates and synthesizes the results of his experimental findings, observations, reading and discussion. He seeks, and with no mean success, to fit into his picture such varied elements as hypnotism, sleep, genius, trance and "possession," ecstasy, disintegration of personality, phantasms, and sensory and motor automatisms. *Human Personality* (as it is usually, and, some say, significantly abbreviated) rapidly earned universal recognition as *the* great standard work of psychical research, a position which it maintains to this day.

Before passing to the next chapter, I think it will be helpful to note a few of the special terms, and the special connotations of some more common ones, found in the terminology of parapsychology.*

Clairvoyance and *telepathy* we have already met, and both of these are classed as types of *extra-sensory perception,* usually abbreviated to ESP. Others are *precognition,* the cognition of a future

---

*In this book I shall tend to use the term common to the period that I am, at a particular moment, concerned with, referring to the early mesmerists and the later hypnotists; to thought-transference rather than telepathy when describing early experiments made before "telepathy" was coined; to "agent" and "percipient" in early experiments and "experimenter" and "subject" in later ones.

event otherwise than by rational inference, and its converse, *retro-cognition*. *Psychokinesis,* or PK, means the alleged direct effect of mind upon matter, as in "willing" dice to fall with certain faces uppermost.

All these are forms of what are variously known as supernormal phenomena, paranormal phenomena, psychic phenomena, etc., terms to which a number of objections have been raised. Some of these objections, particularly those made on etymological grounds, seem somewhat pedantic, and I do not think their use need be eschewed on that score. The objection that these terms, and also others such as clairvoyance and telepathy, may have irrational associations for some people is, however, a reasonable and important one, and it was to meet the need for a "neutral" expression that the term "psi" (Ψ, the twenty-third letter of the Greek alphabet) was introduced. First suggested by two leading British parapsychologists, Drs. Thouless and Wiesner,[6] the term *psi phenomena* is now universally employed as a generic description.

REFERENCES

1. Barrett, William Fletcher: *Psychical Research.* London, 1911.
2. *Report on Spiritualism of the London Dialectical Society.* London, 1871.
3. Podmore, Frank: *Modern Spiritualism.* London, 1902.
4. Barrett, William Fletcher: *Psychical Research.* London, 1911.
5. Sidgwick, Henry *et al.*: Report on the census of hallucinations, *Proc. SPR, 10*: Part 26.
6. Thouless, R. H.: *Proc. SPR, 157*: Part 166.

Chapter 2

TELEPATHY

> *"Unless there is a gigantic conspiracy involving some
> thirty University departments all over the world, and
> several hundred highly respectable scientists in various
> fields, many of them originally hostile to the claims of
> the psychical researchers, the only conclusion the
> unbiased observer can come to must be that there does
> exist a small number of people who obtain knowledge
> existing either in other people's minds or in the outer
> world, by means as yet unknown to science."*
>
> H. J. EYSENCK

TELEPATHY, "the communication of impressions of any kind from one mind to another, independently of the recognized channels of sense," as Myers defined it, or thought-transference, as the early researchers termed it, is certainly the best known and most widely accepted of all forms of paranormal phenomena. There are a number of reasons for this, chief among them being the facts that: (a) it seems to occur much more often than any other form of psi—few people have not at one time or another had experiences in which it seemed that some kind of telepathic process was involved, (b) it is the least difficult form of psi to demonstrate experimentally, and consequently the form to which most research has been devoted, and (c) the layman finds it easier to accept than any other sort of psi, partly by thinking of it as loosely analogous with radio, television and similar forms of modern communication. When we discuss later some of the many theories that have been offered in explanation of telepathy I hope to show the fallaciousness of this last conception.

Investigations into telepathy, and indeed into most forms of psi phenomena, can be generally divided into two categories, (a) the checking and, if possible, verification of reports of its spontaneous occurrence, and (b) the conducting of experiments designed to produce it under controlled conditions. In both cases the person from whom the idea "telepathized" emanates is usually known as the *agent,* while the person upon whom the impression is made is called the *percipient.* The manner of perception may take one of many forms (or a combination of them), the most common being visual, tactile and auditory hallucinations, dreams, "automatic" writing, and probably most familiar, intangible and irrational "hunches."

The sense in which the word "hallucination" is generally used in parapsychology often gives rise to misunderstanding on the part of the newcomer to the subject, and to safeguard against this, and at the same time make clear the meanings of several associated terms, I cannot do better than quote the explanation given by Henry Sidgwick:

"We require some one general term, and the best we can find to include all the species is 'hallucination.' I admit the word to be open to objection, because some people naturally understand from it that the impression so described is entirely false and morbid. But I need not say . . . that this is not our view [the SPR's]. Many of these experiences—though doubtless they all involve some disturbance of the normal action of the nervous system—have no traceable connection with disease of any kind; and a certain number are, as we hold, reasonably regarded as *veridical* or truth telling; they imply in the percipient a capacity above the normal, of receiving knowledge under certain rare conditions.

"Why then, it may be asked, do we use a term that implies erroneous and illusory belief? I answer, first, because in every experience that we call a hallucination there is an element of erroneous belief, though it may be only momentary, and though it may be the means of communicating a truth that could not otherwise have been known. If I seem to see the form of a friend pass through my room, I must have momentarily the false belief that his physical organism is occupying a portion of the space of my room, though a moment's reflection may convince me that this is not so, and though I may immediately draw the inference that he is passing through a crisis of life some miles off, and this inference may turn out to be true. . . . The word *apparition* is no doubt a neutral word that might be used of all visual experiences of this kind, but it could only be used of visual cases. Usage would not allow us to apply it to apparent sounds, or apparent touches. I think then, that we must use 'hallucinations of the senses' as a general term, meaning simply to denote by it a sensory effect, which we cannot attribute to any external physical cause of the kind which would ordinarily produce this effect."

As we have noted, one of the principal reasons for the founding of the SPR was the investigation of telepathy, and *Phantasms of the Living,* and the "Census of Hallucinations," already mentioned (pp. 10-12), contain many well attested examples of spontaneous telepathy. The most striking of these have been cited *ad nauseum,* and will not be repeated here. The two cases now to be quoted, both from *Phantasms of the Living,* are selected as being well authenticated, evidential, and concise. Note the strong emotional factor which is a common characteristic.

In the first case the following statement was made *viva voce* to Edmund Gurney:

"On September 9, 1848, at the siege of Mooltan, my husband, Major-General Richardson, C. B., then adjutant of his regiment, was most severely and dangerously wounded, and supposing himself to be dying, asked one of the officers with him to take the ring off his finger and send it to his wife, who, at that time, was fully 150 miles distant, at Ferozepore. On the night of September 9, 1848, I was lying on my bed, between sleeping and waking, when I distinctly saw my husband being carried off the field, seriously wounded, and heard his voice saying, "Take this ring off my finger, and send it to my wife.' All the next day I could not get the sight or the voice out of my mind. In due time I heard of General Richardson having been severely wounded in the assault on Mooltan. He survived, however, and is still living. It was not for some time after the siege that I heard from Colonel L., the officer who helped to carry General Richardson off the field, that the request as to the ring was actually made to him, just as I had heard it at Ferozepore at that very time. (Signed) M. A. RICHARDSON."[1]

Gurney afterwards obtained confirmation of this report from General Richardson. Myers, who was strongly impressed with this case, comments, "The detail about the ring seems fairly to raise the case out of the category of mere visions of absent persons who are known to be in danger, and with whom the percipient's thoughts have been anxiously engaged."

The second case was reported in a letter, dated December 29, 1883, from a Mrs. Stella, of Chieri, Italy.

"On the 22nd of May, 1882, I was sitting in my room working with other members of my family, and we were talking of household matters, when suddenly I heard the voice of my eldest son calling repeatedly, 'Mamma.' I threw down my work exclaiming, 'There is Nino,' and went downstairs, to the astonishment of everyone. Now my son was at that time in London, and had only left home about a fortnight before, for a two month's tour, so naturally we were all surprised to think he had arrived so suddenly. On reaching the hall, no one was there, and they all laughed at my imagination. But I certainly heard him call, not only once, but three or four times, impatiently. I learnt, a few days afterwards, that on that day he had been taken ill at the house of some friends, and that he had frequently expressed a wish that I should come and nurse him, as not speaking English he could not make himself understood."

On inquiry, Mrs. Stella stated that she had never had any other experiences of this kind. Corroboration of her story was obtained from a lady who had been present at the time. Writing from Breslau, Germany, on February 18, 1884, she stated:

"Mrs. Stella asked me to give you an account of an episode which occured in my presence, while on a visit to her two years ago; and the following are the facts as nearly as I can remember them. We were sitting working together, when Mrs. Stella said she heard the voice of her son, who was absent in England at the time, calling her. This caused us some surprise, as he was not expected home, nor had we heard any sounds of his arrival.

"On going downstairs to meet him, we found no one, which astonished us, as Mrs. Stella had been so positive that she had heard him call. We afterwards heard that on that day he had been taken ill in London. I may here remark that young Mr. Stella is very much attached to his mamma, and especially dependent upon her in sickness. (Signed) CLARA SCHMIDT."[2]

We have noted that "an investigation of the evidence on behalf of thought-transference" was one of the first tasks to which the SPR applied itself. Sir William Barrett had already been experimenting with the daughters of a clergyman named Creery, and claimed considerable success. He interested Myers, Gurney and Sidgwick, who were also impressed. The girls showed marked success at guessing the names of various articles and the suits and numbers of playing cards. The experimenters took what they considered to be ample precautions against cheating, and published a favorable report.[3] Five years later, however, at some tests with Professor and Mrs. Sidgwick (herself a justly famous researcher in her own right), two of the girls were caught attempting to cheat with a simple code, and one of them confessed to having cheated occasionally on previous occasions.[4] Sidgwick, Myers and Gurney thereupon declined to publish any further results or continue with these experiments. Some have claimed that the earlier experiments were invalidated, but Sir William Barrett, in particular, strongly denied this, saying:

"Professor Sidgwick, together with Mr. Myers and Mr. Gurney . . . no doubt considered that at such an elementary stage of the investigation, with as yet so small a quantity of evidence to lay before so many hostile critics, it was absolutely necessary to shun even the appearance of the slightest contact with detected fraud. Under the changed conditions of the present day, however, there is no longer any reason for setting aside the, as I believe, unimpeachable experiments in the earlier stages."[5]

Contemporaneously with the Creery experiments, but quite independently, some trials of a rather different kind were being carried out in Liverpool by Malcolm Guthrie and James Birchall. Their object was the "transference" of sensations, such as tastes and pains, from agent to percipient. Many of the early mesmerists had claimed that they were able to accomplish this "community of sensation" with certain entranced subjects, and Guthrie and Birchall sought to obtain similar results without the use of hypnotism. Myers, Gurney and Barrett were also witnesses at some of these experiments. The procedure was as follows:

Twenty different substances, each with a distinctive taste, were put into parcels or bottles and kept out of sight of the percipient, care being taken to prevent any of their odors from reaching her. As an additional precaution, the use of strong smelling substances was avoided. The percipient would sit with her back to the agent and blindfolded, and the agent would go out of the room, put a small quantity of one of the substances in his mouth, return to the room and place his hand on the percipient's shoulder. The percipient would then tell the experimenters what she seemed to taste. Sometimes she would name the actual substance, while at others she would describe the sensation—thus, with vinegar she said she felt "a sharp and nasty taste." In this way she correctly identified Worcester sauce, bitter aloes, nutmeg, cloves, alum, pepper and acid lozenges.

Similar success was obtained with "transference" of minor pains, inflicted upon themselves by the agents. In these tests, no contact was made between agent and percipient, who nevertheless was correct in localizing the pains ten times and nearly correct six times out of a total of twenty trials. At a further series, in which Sir Oliver Lodge also took part, the percipient identified, with astonishing accuracy, colors, objects, imaginary scenes and rough drawings. She was also successful, when two agents each concentrated on a different object, in identifying both. In the case of the drawings the percipient also made a rough sketch of her impressions. These sketches, which are most convincing, are reproduced side by side with the originals in Myers's *Human Personality*. In many of them the likenesses are so close that any "lucky guessing" explanation is quite unthinkable. Out of a total of 437 trials with tastes, pains, numbers, objects, colors, drawings, etc., 237 were completely successful and several others partly so.[6]

Next, chronologically, come the famous and controversial "Brighton experiments," in which Professor and Mrs. Sidgwick played important parts. As these involved the use of hypnosis, I shall deal with them under the chapter devoted to that subject. I have deferred a number of other cases to that chapter for the same reason.

An important step forward was made in 1905 when two members of the SPR, Miss C. Miles and Miss H. Ramsden, began experiments in telepathy *at a distance*. Miss Miles, who acted as the agent, travelled extensively in England and on the Continent, while Miss Ramsden was living in Buckinghamshire, about twenty miles from London, for part of the time and in Scotland for the rest. Miss Miles, at the time of each experiment, noted in a book the idea she wished to convey, while Miss Ramsden wrote down the impressions she received and sent her record to Miss Miles, who pasted them in the book opposite her own notes, adding explanatory notes of her circumstances at the time. Whenever possible, confirmatory evidence was obtained from independent persons and noted also. Typical examples are now given.

Miss Miles, in London, noticed a man wearing a peculiar pair of spectacles, and on returning home wrote in her book, "October 27, Spectacles—C. M.," making no effort to visualize the object. The same evening in Buckinghamshire, Miss Ramsden wrote, "October 27, 7 p.m. Spectacles. This was the only idea that came to me after waiting a long time.—H. R."

Miss Miles, in London, wrote down, "November 2, Hands." Miss Ramsden in Buckinghamshire, noted "November 2, 7 p.m. I began to visualize a little black hand, well formed."

Similar results were obtained while Miss Ramsden was living in Inverness-shire, Scotland, and Miss Miles was in Bristol, over four hundred miles away. The most striking success, however, was achieved when Miss Miles went to stay at Newbury, Berkshire, also several hundred miles from Miss Ramsden's home in Scotland. Miss Miles's landlady had an invalid daughter in whom Miss Miles became very interested. Without being even aware of this child's existence, Miss Ramsden sent a postcard to Miss Miles saying, "October 31, 1907. I think you wish me to see a little girl with brown hair down her back, tied with a ribbon in the usual way. She is sitting with her back turned and seems busy . . . cutting out scraps with a pair of scissors. She has on a white pinafore, and I should guess her age to be between eight and twelve." A confirmatory letter from the child's mother read, "I have a little girl, aged eleven, with brown hair tied with a ribbon; she wears a pinafore and, being ill, amuses herself by cutting out scraps. I had a long talk (about her) with Miss Miles on October 31.—L. LOVEGROVE."[7]

Results were rarely of this standard, of course, and many of the experiments were failures, but here the comment of Sir William Barrett is pertinent: "When one thinks of the thousands of things that might be selected for the purpose of the experiment, the fact of *any* agreement between the two records is suggestive, but when we find frequent remarkable agreements, the only inference is that one mind must in some way have communicated its impressions to the other."

Experiments in telepathy at a distance were also being carried out at this time by two independent workers, Usher and Burt. In these tests the agent was at Bristol and the percipient in London. Various trials were made with diagrams, but the really important series consisted of thirty trials with playing cards, six trials being made on each of five consecutive evenings. Although only two completely correct "hits" were scored, and the experiments do not appear at first sight to be impressive, they are of importance in that full details of the cards drawn and the guesses made are given in the report, from which it is clear that a remarkable proportion of partial successes was scored, i.e., correct number but wrong suit and *vice versa*. At the time, little significance was attached to this, suitable methods of evaluation not having then been evolved, but when Whately Carington, one of the most celebrated of all parapsychologists, analyzed the data many years after, he found that the successes obtained would occur by pure chance only once in about one hundred and ninety such experiments. He also observed a significant decline in scoring from the first evening to the last, the odds against this occurring by chance being about 175 to one.[8] Carington, a most cautious and critical worker, stated that this case had struck him as extremely convincing.[9]

In 1915, Professor Gilbert Murray, the famous author, playwright and classical scholar, during his Presidential Address to the SPR, surprised his audience by disclosing that he himself had attained considerable success in some telepathic experiments which he had arranged with members of his own family, and related experiences "where the subconscious impression chose some sense-channel by which to reach me."[10] He discovered his thought-reading faculty accidentally through playing guessing games with his wife and children. Mrs. A. W. Verrall, another prominent member of the SPR, made a detailed report to that society in 1916.[11]

Murray's usual procedure was, in his own words, this:

"I go out of the room and of course out of earshot. Someone

in the room, generally my eldest daughter, thinks of a scene or an incident or anything she likes, and says it aloud. It is written down, and I am called. I come in, usually take my daughter's hand, and then, if I have luck, describe in detail what she has thought of. The least disturbance of our customary method, change of time or place, presence of strangers, controversy, and especially noise, is apt to make things go wrong. I become myself somewhat over-sensitive and irritable, though not, I believe, to a noticeable degree."[12]

The subject matter of Murray's experiments, which extended from 1910 to 1920, ranged from incidents in the lives of those taking part to scenes from history and fiction, and imaginary events thought up especially for the experiments. Of the following examples, some were given by Professor Murray himself, others by Mrs. Verrall. The replies are all *verbatim*.

Subject: (by Murray's daughter) Grandfather at the Harrow and Winchester cricket match, dropping hot cigar-ash on Miss Thompson's parasol.

Answer: "Why, this is grandfather. He's at a match—why, it's absurd: He seems to be dropping ashes on a lady's parasol."

Subject: A scene in a story by Strindberg. A man and woman in a lighthouse, the man lying fallen on the floor, and the woman bending over him, looking at him and hoping that he is dead.

Answer: "A horrid atmosphere, full of hatred and discomfort. A book, not real life. A book I have not read. Not Russian, not Italian, but foreign. I cannot get it. There is a round tower, a man and a woman in a round tower; but it is not Maeterlinck. Not like him. I should guess it was Strindberg. The woman is bending over him and hating him, hoping he is dead."

Subject: Miss Barbara Tchaikowsky visiting a political prisoner in the Peter and Paul prison.

Answer: Tchaikowsky, but I can't see what he's doing. No, I've got it blurred. I've got it mixed up with Miss Tchaikowsky. I've got her knocking at a front door."

Subject: Mr. B. putting a tin bath at the top of a staircase.

Answer: "This is Harold B. I thought he was looking in at a shop window, but now I can only get tin pans."

. Many similar successes were achieved, and the number of

partial successes was also high. Some further experiments with Professor Murray were reported in 1923 by Mrs. Henry Sidgwick, who described them as "perhaps the most important ever brought to the notice of the Society."[13] Murray at first attributed his success to auditory hyperaesthesia, by which, without being consciously aware of it, he was able to hear the "subject" or ("target," as modern parapsychologists would term it) when it was spoken, even in adjoining room. Support was lent to this hypothesis by the fact that in partially successful trials, the errors were of a kind usually caused by mishearing. On some occasions, however, Murray gave correct information not mentioned when the "subject" was spoken. At the time of the experiments, Murray was inclined to favor this hyperaesthesia theory, but later in life stated that the source of his knowledge seemed to be mainly telepathic. It is unfortunate, as Dr. Soal, one of the best-known present-day workers in this field, has pointed out, that no attempt seems to have been made at the time, as could easily have been done, to check whether hyperaesthesia was responsible for Murray's success. I do not think this omission, however, justifies Dr. Soal's contention that "the records published by the SPR are merely the records of a parlor game, and not of a serious investigation,"[14] particularly today (since Dr. Soal made this statement) when similar objections have been levelled at some of his own recent work, to which I shall refer later.

"Negative" experiments which have often been cited as evidence against the existence of telepathy can sometimes be shown, by modern methods of interpretation, to be not negative at all. This is true, and of particular importance, in the cases of two early American experimenters, Coover and Troland.

Coover's experiments, and the reasons motivating them, are neatly and accurately summed up by Carington:

"In 1912, Stanford University, California, was offered the handsome endowment of £10,000 for the investigation of Psychical Research and cognate subjects. This was not lightly to be rejected, so, despite the then lack of respectability of the subject and manifest searchings of the heart, the offer was accepted and Dr. Coover was appointed to undertake experimental work. In 1917, there appeared at last a large volume[15] of which the most conspicuous features were its bulk (pp. XXIV-641) and the fact that it contained a larger proportion of irrelevant padding than any other work of an ostensibly scientific character that I have ever seen. The actual work amounted to no more than some 14,000 card-guessing etc., trials, which would represent, I suppose, a small month's work by modern standards. The mountain was indeed in travail; but even the mouse was aborted."[16]

Coover only concerned himself with the difference between trials when the agent looked at the test object (usually a playing card) and trials when he did not, and refused to consider any result short of "certainty," which, for some reason, he defined as odds against chance of 50,000 to one. The main experiment, using a pack of playing cards without the twelve court cards, consisted of 100 guesses each by 100 percipients, half with the agent looking at the card and half without. One thousand trials were also made with various persons who, it was thought, might possess some sort of psychic faculty. The "comparison only" method of scoring, which did not allow for the possibility of clairvoyance (the direct extrasensory perception of the objects themselves) showed no significant difference between the two types of trial and on the strength of this Coover declared that "various statistical treatments of the data fail to reveal any cause beyond chance." Carington, in demonstrating this statement to be completely untrue, points out that if all the trials are pooled, a positive result is obtained with odds against chance of more than 200 to one, and then cites the pertinent comment of Dr. R. H. Thouless, another leading parapsychologist, that if the number of trials had been doubled and the same rate of success maintained, even Coover's own preposterous criterion of 50,000 to one against chance would have been reached. Thouless observes, with what Carington calls "admirable restraint," that "Coover's failure to go on is remarkable."[17]

"The point here," concludes Carington, "is that evidence extracted against his will from an avowed sceptic, who has not even noticed that it was there, is in certain respects more compelling than the triumphant achievements of an enthusiast setting out to prove his case."[18]

Troland's experiments at Harvard in 1916 (also under an

endowment), had a similar outcome, although the technique was quite different. The agent looked into a darkened box containing a central illuminated spot, on either side of which could appear an illuminated square, the lighting controlled by a commutator driven by an electric motor. The percipient was required to indicate on which side of the spot the square appeared by pressing a switch that automatically recorded his impression. The trials were divided into two sections, one in which the squares were illuminated for forty seconds each time, and the other for eighty seconds. Surprisingly, after devising such an elaborate apparatus, Troland made only 605 trials, and then abandoned the experiments.

Carington has shown[19] that although the gross scores were not significant—the successes numbering 284 against an expected 301.5 —the forty-second section showed a *negative* score with odds against chance better than twenty to one. Carington observes that "Troland, like Coover, ought to have gone on, but presumably it did not occur to him that it is just as difficult to keep guesses consistently *wrong* in the absence of knowledge of what the test object is, as to keep them consistently right. And again, like Coover, he is rather in the position of a poacher turned gamekeeper without even realizing it, so that errors attendant on excessive enthusiasm may equally be discounted."[20]

We come now to some experiments which many parapsychologists, including both Carington and Soal, regard as by far the most important of all the early work in this field, namely, those carried out in 1920 at Groningen University, Holland, by Heymans, Brugmans and Wynberg. The percipient in all the experiments was a young man named van Dam, and the technique, so far as he was concerned, was always the same. He sat, blindfolded and screened by heavy curtains, facing a board marked out in forty-eight two-inch squares arranged in eight columns of six. The columns were lettered from A to H, and six rows so formed numbered one to six. His task was to point to the square selected by the experimenters, who made their selection by drawing two cards, one from a lettered pack and the other from a numbered one. The percipient was then "willed" to point to the square bearing the corresponding letter and number.

Out of a total of 187 trials van Dam obtained the remarkable score of sixty successes, as against a chance expectation of only four.

To overcome the possible objection that the experimenters might, in the excitement and tenseness of the moment, give away sensory clues, perhaps by an increased rate of breathing or a creak of a chair, they conducted about half their tests from a room immediately above that in which the subject was seated, viewing the board through a small double glazed window in the floor. The trials made in this way were more successful than the others.

Some further interesting information was also gleaned from these experiments. In twenty-four of the trials the subject was first given a dose of bromide, and in twenty-nine a dose of alcohol. The results with bromide were significantly better than those where nothing was given, and those with alcohol even better.[21, 22]

In February, 1927, with the co-operation of the British Broadcasting Corporation, Dr. V. J. Woolley, then Research Officer of the SPR, arranged a mass telepathy experiment in which radio listeners were asked to take part. Five objects were displayed at the SPR headquarters, and Sir Oliver Lodge, in a BBC studio, asked listeners to record their impressions as each object was "willed" by the agents. Three minutes were allowed for each object, with a break of two minutes each time. The only information given to the listeners was that objects one and four were playing cards of unusual design and that object two was a picture. Object two was, in fact, a Japanese print representing a skull surmounted by a bird, object three was a bunch of white lilac, and object five was Dr. Woolley himself, wearing a bowler hat and a grotesque mask. In order to meet possible objections of collusion or leakage in the event of the experiment proving successful, Woolley and the other "agents" remained on the SPR premises all that night, without access to a telephone.

Twenty-four thousand six hundred fifty-nine answers were received from listeners and analyzed. The result showed no clear evidence of telepathy, although Dr. Woolley stated in his report "There does seem to be an indication of a supernormal faculty on the part of a few of those who took part, though their successes are swamped by the very large mass of failures on the part of others."

Although the experiment did not produce positive results of telepathy, it proved of considerable value in demonstrating certain general tendencies in selecting cards; for instance, there were more than three times as many guesses of five as of six (both wrong) and a marked preference was noted for odd as against even cards. There was a strong tendency to choose an ace, particularly the ace of spades. These are factors to be considered, of course, in assessing chance probability in parapsychological experiments, when using playing cards or cards bearing numbers.[23]

In America, one of the best organized and workmanlike experiments of this period was made at Harvard in 1925-6 by George H. Estabrooks, with college students as subjects. Ordinary playing cards were used in all the trials, which were divided into two groups. In the first of these, experimenters and subjects were respectively in the two halves of a large room divided by closed double doors, the instructions when to "guess" being conveyed by an electrical signalling system. Eighty-three trials, each of twenty guesses, were made on the colors of the cards, with convincingly positive results; 938 correct out of the 1,660 as against a chance expectation of 830, or odds better than over ten million to one against chance. In the second group of trials the experimenters and subjects were in different rooms about sixty feet apart, and this time results were significantly below chance expectation. Out of a total of 640 guesses (thirty-two sets of twenty) only 130 successes in guessing the suit of the card were scored against a chance expectation of 160, representing odds against chance of about 100 to one.

Unfortunately, these experiments were not continued further, partly owing to the difficulty in obtaining sufficient new subjects and partly, according to Carington, "because Dr. Estabrooks did not fully realize that below-chance scores are just as interesting, and just as indicative of some peculiar factor at work, as are above-chance scores; indeed, they may be of even higher evidential value, because it is so unlikely that, e.g., unwittingly given or gathered clues should work in the wrong direction."[24]

No account of telepathy experiments of this period could fairly omit reference to the American novelist and sociologist, Upton Sinclair, and the astonishing accounts of his own experiences recorded in his book *Mental Radio*.[25] After his wife had given spontaneous evidence of a marked faculty as a percipient, Sinclair staged a series of tests. In most of these, the agent, usually Sinclair himself, sat in one room and concentrated on a drawing, while Mrs. Sinclair, in another, attempted to visualize the picture and draw a reproduction. In some of the tests Mrs. Sinclair was handed the drawings folded, which, in order to obtain her impressions, she held against her solar plexus. In some trials, with her brother-in-law acting as agent, she was apparently successful when a distance of forty miles separated them. An interesting feature of Sinclair's experiments was the frequency with which "near misses" were scored, the percipient drawing something similar in appearance to, but quite unconnected with, the "target" drawing. For instance, in response to a target of an alpine hat she drew something remarkably like it, but which she labelled "chafing dish," and to a crude sketch of a volcano with smoke issuing from the top she responded with an almost identical drawing which she named as a "black beetle." Conversely, Mrs. Sinclair sometimes perceived the correct idea but gave a completely different interpretation of it. Sinclair claims that out of a series of 290 experiments 23 per cent were fully successful, 53 per cent partly successful, and only the remaining 24 per cent complete failures. Here again, it is unfortunate that no properly controlled experiments seem to have been made in the presence of independent observers.

In passing, it is worthy of note that another famous American author, the celebrated Mark Twain, was a pioneer investigator into thought-transference. In 1878, he published a paper entitled *Mental Telegraphy*, in which he described many personal experiences, and seventeen years later a sequel, *More Mental Telegraphy*.

The famous French parapsychologist René Warcollier, late president of the Institut Métapsychique, Paris, devoted many years to the study of telepathy, and his book *Mind to Mind* is one of the modern classics of the subject. His interest was first awakened by a series of telepathic dreams, and in 1920, he organized collective experiments in which groups of agents and percipients attempted to transmit the impressions of drawings, first from room to room, then from one part of Paris to another, and later from city to city and country to country. In many instances, the last named, especially those between France and America, were more successful than the short-distance trials. In addition to drawings, Warcollier experimented, with varying success, in transmitting impressions of printed symbols, cards, the time indicated on a clock face, and other targets. Some of the experiments were made in collaboration with Dr. Gardner Murphy, an equally well known American parapsychologist, who had formed a similar group in the United States. In this connection, Warcollier makes the interesting observation that of the Americans who took part, the most successful were those who had been to Paris and met the French group.

A "follow-up" to the mass telepathy broadcasting experiment already described was made in 1927-8 by Dr. Soal, who arranged for over one hundred of the most promising participants in that experiment to take part in a test of telepathy at a distance, and in 1928-9 he arranged a further series with over five hundred percipients who volunteered in response to a broadcast appeal. The results were not statistically significant but are noteworthy on account of Soal's brilliant analysis.

With the closing years of the 1920's came also the close of another era in psychical research, although few could have foreseen the momentous events which, in the early part of the next decade, were to precipitate the transition of "traditional" psychical research into modern experimental parapsychology. The credit for bringing about this metamorphosis is very largely due to a young botanist (as he then was) Dr. Joseph Banks Rhine. Keenly interested in psychical research, he and his wife, Dr. Louisa E. Rhine, approached the famous psychologist Professor William McDougall, a past president of the SPR, who they knew was also interested, and who was at the time opening a new department of psychology at Duke University, North Carolina. McDougall arranged for them to carry on research at the University under his auspices, and by 1930, experimental work was well in hand. It was not until 1934, however, that Rhine altered the whole picture of psychical research when he "dropped a bombshell into the camp of the sceptics" (as Harry Price puts it)[26] by the publication of *Extra-Sensory Perception*,[27] a report of his early experiments and the sensational results he had obtained. Sensational is, perhaps, an understatement, for the interest aroused and the controversy provoked by this report have never abated, and Rhine and the Parapsychology Laboratory at Duke have become justly famous. And small wonder, for Rhine's results, using new methods which lent themselves to accurate analysis, and obtained under conditions of rigorous control, seemed, by all previous standards, little short of miraculous. We shall return to the consideration of the work of Rhine and his associates in a later chapter.

REFERENCES

1. Gurney, Edmund, Myers, F. W. H., and Podmore, Frank: *Phantasms of the Living*. London, 1886.
2. Ibid.
3. Ibid.
4. See *Proc. SPR, 5*:269.
5. Barrett, William Fletcher: *Psychical Research*. London, 1911.
6. Guthrie, Malcolm: An account of some experiments in thought-transference, *Proc. SPR, 2*: Part 5, see also *3*: Part 9.
7. Miles, Clarissa, and Ramsden, Hermione: Experiments in thought-transference, *Proc. SPR, 21*: Part 54.
8. Usher, F. L., and Burt, F. P.: *Annales des Seances Psychiques*. Vol. 20, 1910.
9. Carington, W. Whately: *Telepathy*. London, 1945.
10. Murray, George Gilbert Aime: Presidential address, *Proc. SPR, 29*: Part 72.
11. Verral, A. W.: Report on a series of experiments in "guessing," *Proc. SPR, 29*: Part 72.
12. Ibid.
13. Sidgwick, Eleanor: Report on some recent experiments in thought-transference carried out by Professor Murray, *Proc. SPR, 34*: Part 92.
14. Soal, S. G.: *Experimental Telepathy and Clairvoyance in England*. London, 1933.
15. Coover, John E.: *Experiments in Psychical Research*. Stanford University, 1917.
16. Carington, W. Whately: *Telepathy*. London, 1945.
17. Thouless, R. H.: *Proc. SPR, 43*: Part 139.
18. Carington, W. Whately: *Telepathy*. London, 1945.

19. Ibid.
20. Ibid.
21. Brugmans, H. J. F. W.: *Compte-Rendu du Premier Congres International des Recherches Psychiques a Copenhague.* 1921.
22. Soal, S. G.: *Experimental Telepathy and Clairvoyance in England.* London, 1933.
23. Woolley, V. J.: The broadcasting experiment in mass telepathy, *Proc. SPR, 38*: Part 105.
24. Carington, W. Whately: *Telepathy.* London, 1945.
25. Sinclair, Upton: *Mental Radio.* Illinois, 1930.
26. Price, Harry: *Fifty Years of Psychical Research.* London, 1939.
27. Rhine, Joseph Banks: *Extra-Sensory Perception.* Boston, 1934.

Chapter 3

CLAIRVOYANCE

"We are living in the Marvellous, in that which
stretches beyond the limits in which we live,
beyond death and beyond birth."

JEAN COCTEAU

THE WORD "clairvoyance" is correctly used in parapsychology to signify "the extra-sensory perception of *objective events* as distinguished from telepathic cognition of the mental activities of another person." Although they would not have defined it in such sophisticated language, this is the sense in which the early mesmerists and "magnetizers" used the term, long before the advent of modern spiritualism; but confusion now often arises through its misapplication in describing certain spiritualist activities. In newspaper and other announcements of spiritualist meetings one reads of "demonstrations of clairvoyance," or sees notices such as "speaker so-and-so, clairvoyant such-and-such," or even, to quote an actual example, "The evening of clairvoyance . . . has had to be cancelled owing to unforeseen circumstances."[1] It will be seen that "clairvoyance" in such contexts is meant to describe the process whereby a "medium" gives purporting messages from the dead, a sense quite at variance with the definition given above. This appropriation by the spiritualist "movement" of a word already bearing an established meaning in psychical research is the cause of much confusion and misunderstanding. It is, I hope, unnecessary to explain that in this book I invariably use "clairvoyance" in the sense defined at the beginning of this paragraph.

This possible confusion of meaning is, however, a minor problem compared with the difficulty of establishing whether a given phenomenon is, in fact, clairvoyance. In some of the cases I shall quote, it would certainly be possible to suggest that the relevant matter might have been in somebody's mind, so that telepathy, albeit with an unwitting "agent," is a possible explanation. Devising ways of eliminating this possibility and isolating clairvoyance experimentally is a problem that has taxed the ingenuity of some of our finest workers, and much time and effort have been applied to this problem. Let us say then, that here are some examples of psi phenomena in which it appears, *prima facie,* that the process is a clairvoyant rather than a telepathic one.

By far the most famous possessor of a (presumably) clairvoyant faculty was the celebrated Swedish mystic, Emanuel Swedenborg (1688-1782), and few have not heard, in one version or another, the story of his extraordinary description of the progress of the great fire at Stockholm on July 29, 1759. Here is the true account, as given by an equally celebrated contemporary of Swedenborg, the great philosopher, Immanuel Kant. Swedenborg arrived, direct from England, at 4 p.m. on that day, to join a party of guests at the house of a friend, William Castel, at Gottenburg, which is three hundred miles from Stockholm. Kant wrote:

"About six o'clock Swedenborg went out, and returned to the company quite pale and alarmed. He said that a dangerous fire had just broken out in Stockholm, at the Södermalm, and that it was spreading very fast. He said that the house of one of his friends, whom he named, was already in ashes; and that his own was in danger. At eight o'clock, after he had been out again, he joyfully exclaimed, 'Thank God! the fire is extinguished; the third door from my house!' This news occasioned great commotion throughout the whole city . . . It was announced to the Governor the same evening. On Sunday morning Swedenborg was summoned to the Governor, who questioned him concerning the disaster. Swedenborg described the fire precisely, how it had begun and in what manner it had ceased, and how long it had continued. On the same day the news spread through the city, and as the Governor thought it worthy of attention, the consternation was considerably increased; because many were in trouble on account of their friends and property . . . On Monday evening a messenger arrived at Gottenburg, who was dispatched by the Board of Trade during the time of the fire. In the letters brought by him, the fire was described precisely in the manner stated by Swedenborg. On Tuesday a Royal Courier arrived at the Governor's with the melancholy intelligence of the fire, of the losses which it had occasioned, and of the houses it had damaged and ruined, not in the least differing from that which Swedenborg had given at the very time when it happened; for the fire was extinguished at eight o'clock."[2]

Telepathy from the minds of actual witnesses of the fire? Possibly, of course, but if clairvoyance is demonstrated to be a fact, it becomes the simplest hypothesis. In the next case, also recorded by Kant, who went to great pains to verify the incident, clairvoyance (or, as Swedenborg claimed, a message from the dead) seems, on the face of it, the only possible explanation.

"Madame Hertville (Martville), the widow of the Dutch Ambassador in Stockholm, some time after the death of her husband, was called upon by Croon, a goldsmith, to pay for a silver service which her husband had purchased from him. The widow was convinced that her late husband had been much too precise and orderly not to have paid this debt, yet she was unable to find the receipt. In her sorrow, and because the amount was considerable, she requested Swedenborg to call at her house. After apologizing to him for troubling him, she said that if, as all people say, he possessed the extraordinary gift of conversing with the souls of the departed, he would perhaps have the kindness to ask her husband how it was about the silver service. Swedenborg did not at all object to comply with her request. Three days afterwards, the said lady had company at her house for coffee. Swedenborg called and in his cool way informed her that he had conversed with her husband. The debt had been paid several months before his decease, and the receipt was in a bureau in the room upstairs. The lady replied that the bureau had been quite cleared out, and that the receipt was not found among all the papers. Swedenborg said that her husband had described to him how, after pulling out the left-hand drawer, a board would appear, which required to be drawn out, when a secret compartment would be disclosed, containing his private Dutch correspondence as well as the receipt. Upon hearing this description the whole company arose and accompanied the lady into the room upstairs. The bureau was opened; they did as they were directed; the compartment was found, of which no one had ever known before; and to the great astonishment of all, the papers were discovered there, in accordance with his description."[3]

I shall discuss in a later chapter whether this and similar cases offer sufficient evidence for a belief in communication with the spirits of the dead. Suffice it here to say that many cases claimed by some to support such a belief can be more readily and simply explained as clairvoyance or telepathy. While on the subject of spirit communication, it will be well to make clear the sense in which another word associated with spiritualism is used in parapsychology, namely "medium" and of course, its derivatives "mediumship" and such terms as "mediumistic phenomena." In spiritualistic usage, a medium is one through whom the spirits of the dead are claimed to communicate. Parapsychology, of course, is not committed to such a belief, and when we refer to a certain "medium" we really mean, "someone who produces or whose presence assists in the production of certain forms of psi phenomena, claimed by some as evidence of communication, etc." Thus a "genuine" medium is one who actually produces psi phenomena (as distinct from one who "fakes" them) whatever his own belief as to the nature and cause of the phenomena. We speak normally of a "medium"—one who claims or appears to produce psi phenomena (but who perhaps never has), and a "fraudulent medium" —one who has been proved to cheat (although *possibly* able sometimes to produce genuine phenomena).

Clairvoyance (we will take "seeming," "alleged" and similar qualifications as read) can take place in a number of ways and under a variety of conditions. The traditional crystal ball, a blot of ink, a pool of water or heap of sand—any "neutral" object upon which attention can be focussed—assists certain persons in achieving the state of mild dissociation sometimes necessary for "seeing" in this way. Sometimes known as "scrying," this method is one of the oldest and best known. Sitting passively and quietly until a rather different condition, often called a "brown study," is induced, will sometimes bring about hallucinations, visual or auditory, which can, it seems, sometimes be veridical. Some people fall spontaneously into a state in which visions are seen and voices heard, others in similar circumstances can hold a pencil, and produce, without conscious effort, "automatic" writing and drawings. Some degree of dissociation, ranging from a slight "not with us" condition to deep trance, or autohypnosis, is usually present. Many of the best attested examples of clairvoyance have been observed in hypnotized subjects, and I shall deal with these, as with the case of telepathy in hypnosis, in a special chapter. Instances of clairvoyance also occur in the drowsy "hypnagogic" state immediately preceding sleep, and the similar "hypnopompic" condition between sleeping and waking, before one is fully awake. Far more frequently reported, however, are clairvoyant *dreams*, of which I shall now give some examples.

On March 22, 1903, a man was drowned in the river Severn near Kidderminster, Worcester, and it was not until several days later that his body was found. The report of the inquest in the local newspaper included the following: " . . . Thomas Butler, who found the body, said it was owing to a dream the night before that he visited the spot where he found the body. It was six miles from the scene of the fatality. A verdict of 'Accidentally drowned' was returned, the coroner remarking on the curious circumstances of the dream . . . Thomas Butler, laborer, of Beel Row, Stourport, said on Wednesday morning he went towards Shrawley Wood. On the previous evening he dreamt that he saw the body of a man on the top side of the Lincombe Weir. He went for a walk with a man, and told him that he had had the dream. They went round Shrawley Wood and returned by Hamstall Hotel, and when just below Lincombe Weir he saw the body of a man in the water in the Weir cutting. He got a boat and called to John Oakley, clerk at the Lincombe Lock, who said that a policeman was at the lockhouse. Witness rowed the boat across the river, picked up Police Constable Meaks, and took him to the spot where the body was. They put the body into the boat, and it was conveyed to the mortuary."

"*The Coroner:* 'Are you in the habit of having these realistic dreams?'

"*Witness:* 'No, sir.'

"*The Coroner:* 'You might be a useful man if you were.'

"*Witness:* 'Very likely, sir.' "

A representative of the SPR, Colonel Taylor, made a careful investigation afterwards, and reported that the dead man had been seen to fall into the river, but the strong current had carried him away before any attempt at rescue could be made. Several local people told Colonel Taylor that the place where the body was found was a most unlikely one, and this indicated strongly that Butler had not just made a lucky guess. The landlord of an hotel where Butler had called before finding the body confirmed that Butler had related the dream not only to him, but to several others, and had stated that he was going to look about at Lincombe for the body. Oddly, in his dream Butler had seen the body caught in some bushes below the Weir, whereas it was actually found, in exactly the same circumstances, but caught in some bushes above the Weir.

Here is a more recent, and even more dramatic, case of clairvoyance during a dream. Like the one just described, it was checked very thoroughly by officers of the SPR.

On June 27, 1928, Mr. Dudley F. Walker, of Stoughton, near Guildford, Surrey, had a vivid dream in which he seemed to witness a terrible railway accident. At the commencement of his dream he seemed to be in a railway signal box at night, over a line that he had never seen before (Mr. Walker was not in any way connected with railways). A train was approaching, which in some way he knew to be an express excursion, full of people returning from some function. He felt somehow that "the train was doomed," and then found himself "hovering in the air" and following the train, which was slowing as it approached a station. Then he was horrified to see another train coming in the opposite direction on the same line, and although they both seemed to be travelling fairly slowly there was a violent collision. He saw the express locomotive and its coaches "pitch and twist" in the air with a terrific noise.

Later, he seemed to be walking beside the wreckage in the light of dawn, "viewing with a feeling of terror the huge, over-turned engine and smashed coaches." The scene was one of "inde-scribable horror"; bodies, most of them of women and girls, lying beside the track, and the body of a man in a ghastly state, on the side of an overturned coach. He heard a doctor say, "Poor chap, he's dead," and another person's voice saying he thought he had seen the eyelids move, to which the doctor replied, "It's only your nerves, he has been dead some time."

Walker awoke early next morning feeling too upset and unwell to eat his breakfast, and recounted the dream to his mother, who in turn told his sister while he was dressing. On arriving at his place of business he told the managing director of his firm about the dream, and also noted it in his diary.

When leaving his office later in the day, he was astonished to see all the newspaper placards announcing a serious railway accident which had happened at Darlington, over two hundred and fifty miles away, on the previous night at about the same time as he had experienced his dream. He was even more amazed when, on reading the reports of the crash, he discovered that they corresponded in a number of details with the events in his dream. Here is part of the account in the *Northern Echo* of June 28, 1928:

"A terrible railway accident occurred just before midnight last night outside Darlington Bank Top Station.

"A Newcastle-Scarborough excursion, returning to Newcastle, collided at about 11:20 with an express goods train for London from the north. The excursion train was full of trippers.

"It was learnt at 3:00 this morning that at least eight people were killed and about thirty injured. The eight bodies are those of a man, six women, and one little girl . . .

"The trains crashed with great force. Two coaches of the excursion train were telescoped and the engine of one of the trains was completely derailed and lay broadside on to the track.

"There were distressing scenes . . . One gruesome sight was that of a man's body lying on top of one of the carriages . . . "

Mr. Walker, who had never previously experienced any sort of veridical dream, was so puzzled that he wrote letters containing detailed accounts to the *Daily Mail* and to the *Surrey Advertiser*, hoping that others might be interested or able to explain it. The Rev. A. T. Fryer, seeing the published letter, immediately wrote to Mr. Walker on behalf of the SPR asking for further information. With his reply Mr. Walker sent statements from his mother, his sister, and his managing director, all testifying that they had been told in detail about the dream before Mr. Walker learned of the

Darlington crash in the newspapers. Further correspondence also elicited the following additional information.

Mr. Walker had never had a similar dream. He had never been to Darlington or anywhere near to it, and did not know anyone who lived there or was connected in any way with the town. He made an entry in his diary the morning after his dream with a sketch showing how the two trains in his dream had collided. He had no experience whatsoever of railway work, and nothing at all had occurred on the day of his dream which might have made him think of railways, by which he seldom travelled. The dream seemed to have been in two parts, the first at the time of the accident or thereabouts, and the second much later in the night; he remembered waking between the two parts. He had never before to his recollection dreamt of any kind of violent accident—in fact, it was a subject of remark in his family that he was such an infrequent dreamer.

"It made," said Mr. Walker, "a deep impression on my mind, and although I have never given serious thought to this subject, I am now perfectly convinced that this was no ordinary dream. It was so remarkably true to life that it seemed more like a vision of events taking place, than the average dream." Not unnaturally, he asked, "Why should I, out of all the millions in England asleep at that time, be picked out to witness this ghastly sight?"[4] I wish I could tell him.

No less an authority than William James, "the most renowned of the thinkers of America"[5] and a past president of both the English and American Societies for Psychical Research, was responsible for the report of the following striking example of trance clairvoyance. On Monday, October 31, 1898, a young girl disappeared from her home in Enfield, New Hampshire. She was last seen crossing a bridge over a lake. An intense search of the shore of the lake and some nearby woods was made, and for two days a diver searched vainly for her body.

On the day before the girl disappeared, Mrs. Titus, a nonprofessional "medium" living at Lebanon, some four miles from the girl's home, told her husband she had a presentiment that "something awful was going to happen," and on the Monday morning declared that it had happened. At midday her husband, who worked with the girl's sister at a mill, told Mrs. Titus that this sister had gone home, he imagined because her mother was ill. In the evening they heard that the girl, whom they did not know, was missing.

The following day, Mrs. Titus affirmed that the girl was in the lake and this, of course, was no more than a natural supposition. On the Wednesday evening, however, she fell into a trance, and when awakened by her husband said that if he had left her she would have discovered the girl's whereabouts. Later that evening she went into another trance, during which she said that she could see the girl standing on a frost-covered log on the bridge, that her foot had slipped and she had fallen back into the lake. The body, she said, was lying in a certain place, which she described, by the bridge, between two logs and covered with mud. One foot, with a new rubber shoe on it, was projecting.

The next morning, Mr. Titus related the facts of his wife's trance visions to some workmates, and his foreman gave him permission to take Mrs. Titus to the bridge. She quickly identified the place seen during her trance, but no body was visible. On telling their story to a local mill-owner, a Mr. Whitney who had organized the search, he returned to the bridge with them, and instructed the diver to search at the spot pointed out by the medium. Sure enough, he found the body, lying exactly as she had "seen" it.

In William James's report, the testimonies of Whitney and the diver are given in detail. That of the diver confirms also that the body was lying at a depth of about eighteen feet, and that the water was so dark that he could see nothing, but found the body by feeling for it. It was also established that Mrs. Titus had not been to the bridge for two years or more previous to the tragedy, nor did she visit the spot after her trance vision until the morning when the body was found.[6]

There is another important form of clairvoyance that I have not so far mentioned, namely object-reading or *psychometry*. Some persons, when given an object to hold, are able to describe events and persons connected with the object. Similar results are sometimes obtained with photographs or letters in sealed envelopes.

The word psychometry was first used in this sense by an American, Dr. J. Rodes Buchanan (1814-1898) in 1842. He claimed to have been successful, not only in the experimental demonstration of object-reading, but in the treatment of patients by a similar technique, averring that certain of them derived as much benefit from holding a sealed bottle (without knowing what it contained) of a particular medicine as from taking it in the normal way.[7]

Literally signifying "soul-reading," the word, although possibly in accord with Buchanan's quaint theories, is an unfortunate choice, particularly today when it is employed in experimental psychology[8] in quite a different sense and with greater regard for its etymology. It has, however, attained such wide currency as a synonym for object-reading that there would now be little point in changing it.

There would appear to be two somewhat distinct forms of psychometry, one in which the "sensitive" perceives events directly connected with the object, such events usually being in the (sometimes remote) past, and the other in which the object seems to form a telepathic link between the mind of the sensitive and that of a person or persons connected with it. In this case the object appears to serve no further purpose once this nexus has been established.

A contemporary of Buchanan, Professor William Denton, a Boston geologist, carried out numerous experiments which, he claimed, confirmed Buchanan's findings. In the majority of his tests the "sensitive" was his sister, Mrs. Anna Denton Cridge. This lady could, it was said, describe in detail the appearance, character and environment of the writer of a letter by holding it, in a sealed envelope, against her forehead.

In one notable experiment, when given a piece of lava from the Kilauea volcano in Hawaii she declared, "I see the ocean and ships sailing on it. This must be an island, for water is all around. Now I am turned from where I saw the vessels, and am looking at something most terrific. It seems as if an ocean of fire were pouring over a precipice, and boiling as it pours. The sight permeates my whole being, and inspires me with terror. I see it flow into the ocean and the water boils intensely." The experience gave her a feeling of terror which persisted for over an hour. Denton's report stresses that she could not, in the normal way, have had any knowledge of the nature and origin of the object.

Various other geological specimens produced equally striking results: for example, a piece of limestone bearing glacial scratches gave her the impression of being frozen in a great mass of ice—"grinding, pressing and rushing along—a mountainous mass." The most remarkable description of all, however, is the one she gave on handling a small piece of a mastodon tooth. " . . . a part of some monstrous animal, probably part of a tooth. I feel like a perfect monster, with heavy legs, unwieldy head, and a very large body. I go down to a shallow stream to drink. I can hardly speak, my jaws are so heavy. I feel like getting down on all fours. What a noise comes through the wood. I have an impulse to answer it. My ears are very large and leathery, and I can almost fancy they flap my face as I move my head. There are some older ones than I. It seems too, so out of keeping to be talking with these heavy jaws. They are dark brown, as if they had been completely tanned. There is one old fellow, with large tusks, that looks very tough. I see several young ones; in fact there is a whole herd."

It is unfortunate (the cynic might say significant) that these early experimenters did not seem to realize the need for authentication of their work by independent witnesses and the elimination of all possible loopholes. Such objections cannot be levelled, however, at the tests made by Sir Oliver Lodge with the famous American medium, Mrs. Leonore Piper (of whom more later). When she visited England in 1889, Lodge personally escorted her from the liner in order that she might have no opportunity to make contact with any sources of information. She was taken to Cambridge the next day by F. W. H. Myers, at whose house she stayed under the strictest surveillance. Later, when she stayed with Lodge, all her correspondence was supervised, all the household servants were changed, and even the family Bible was locked away. Nevertheless, she gave many convincing demonstrations of her psychic faculty, the following being a typical example.

Sir Oliver Lodge obtained from an uncle a watch which had belonged to that relative's twin brother who had died many years previously. This he gave to Mrs. Piper during a trance sitting. Her "control" straight away stated correctly that it belonged to an uncle named Jerry, who then purported to communicate. "Jerry" gave accounts of a number of childhood incidents, such as killing a cat in a field belonging to a man named Smith, nearly drowning when swimming in a creek, and owning a peculiar skin, which looked like that of a snake. Lodge's uncle, to whom he wrote for verification of these occurrences, replied that he had possessed a snake's skin, but had never killed a cat and could not recall the other incidents. A second brother of the dead man was contacted, and he recalled quite definitely that he had killed a cat, that they frequently played together in Smith's field, and that he had narrowly escaped drowning while swimming in a creek.

In view of the stringent precautions which Lodge took it seems certain that, although the actual source from which Mrs. Piper obtained her information is by no means clear, she could not have obtained it by normal means. It is important also to note that Lodge knew nothing of his uncle's childhood, and had no idea at the time whether the statements made by the medium were correct.

No less strict were the test conditions under which a famous non-professional sensitive, Stephan Ossowiecki, a Polish engineer, demonstrated his amazing psychometric gifts to several leading British and European researchers. Born in 1877, he is said to have inherited his psychic faculty from his mother, and to have practised thought-reading and clairvoyance from an early age. When a student, he astounded his tutors by answering questions written down and enclosed in sealed envelopes, and established a reputation as a finder of lost property.

In the early 1920s, Ossowiecki was tested by Dr. Gustave Geley, then head of the Institut Métapsychique, Paris, and Professor Charles Richet, the famous physiologist and Nobel prizewinner, who was equally eminent in the field of psychical research. Ossowiecki achieved spectacular success at reading the contents of sealed, opaque envelopes, which were sometimes unknown even to the experimenters. A typical reading is that of a phrase written by Geley, from which Ossowiecki obtained impressions of "a fight involving a large animal; an elephant; in water; blood; wounded in the trunk; a fight with a crocodile." What Geley had written was, "An elephant bathing in the Ganges attacked by a crocodile which bit off his trunk."

At Warsaw, in 1921, Ossowiecki accurately described the contents of a lead cylinder, the ends of which had been sealed by soldering. No one present knew what the cylinder contained—a caricature of Marshal Pilsudski, faceless, except for his heavy moustache and prominent eyebrows—it having been prepared by a lady who left Warsaw as soon as she had done so. At first Ossowiecki could only say that it was something original by a lady, but at a second attempt he said the cylinder contained the drawing of a man with a moustache and large eyebrows but without a nose. The face, he said, resembled Pilsudski.

Ossowiecki's most dramatic and convincing demonstration of his clairvoyance, however, was given at the Second International Congress for Psychical Research held in Warsaw, in 1923. The test, which was devised and put into execution by Dr. Eric J. Dingwall, at that time Research Officer of the SPR, was made in the presence of many of Europe's leading psychical researchers. Dr. Dingwall made up a sealed package containing envelopes of various colors, one within the other, the inner one containing a sheet of paper folded in two. On this paper were drawings of a flag and a bottle, the date, August 22, 1923, and a sentence written in French. In order to reduce the chance of telepathy Dr. Dingwall himself was not present when the test was made. On receiving the package Ossowiecki drew the bottle and the flag accurately and read the date correctly except for the month, which he said might be the name of a town. He was unable to read the sentence on the back of the paper, the effort of reading the first part having, he said, made him too tired. He also named the colors of the envelopes correctly. The experiment was hailed as a brilliant success, and drew cheers from those who witnessed it. Baron von Schrenck-Notzing, one of Europe's most respected parapsychologists, is reported to have rushed up to Ossowiecki crying *"Merci, merci, au nom de la science!"*

Turning now to quantitative experimental work, we find that comparatively few experiments were made before 1930 to ascertain whether clairvoyance, as distinct from telepathy, could be demonstrated. The best known are those carried out by Miss Ina Jephson from 1924 onwards.

Miss Jephson's tests were made with ordinary playing cards, using a special system of scoring devised by Professor R. A. Fisher. This system permits successes in color, suit, number, etc., to be combined in a single score. The method used was for the subject to draw a card from the pack face downwards; guess; record the guess; turn the card over and record the actual card; shuffle the cards and then repeat the procedure. Five guesses were made at each of five sittings, giving a total of twenty-five guesses per subject.

The subjects made their guesses at home, using their own packs of cards, and sent their results to Miss Jephson by post. Two hundred and forty subjects sent in a complete series of results, giving a total of 6,000 guesses, made up of 1,200 each of first, second, third, fourth and fifth guesses. Analysis of these scores showed that the overall average score was well above chance expectation, and also that the rate of scoring showed a steady decline from the first guess down to the fourth, rising again at the fifth to almost the same level as the first.

A number of criticisms have been levelled at the Jephson experiments, and not altogether without justification. The "do-it-yourself" technique ruled out any possibility of adequate supervision, and even if we accept (which we are not entitled to do) that all the subjects were honest and of reasonable intelligence, there is always the possibility that, consciously or otherwise, they were guided, to some extent at least, by *points de repère* on the backs of the cards. The importance of the last-mentioned is borne out by the fact that when, at the insistence of Dr. Soal, similar experiments (which he himself analyzed) were made, with the cards enclosed in light-proof envelopes, no deviation from chance expectation was found. On the other hand, an analysis of a small number of the Jephson trials that *were* witnessed showed the same pattern of a significant total score and a significant decline effect, and no less an authority than Whately Carington considers this to be good reason for accepting the general indications of the Jephson experiments as a whole.

The Jephson experiments were concluded at the close of the

1920s: at the end, as we have noted before, of the second great era or phase in psychical research. In discussing the various forms of clairvoyance I have not yet mentioned *precognition,* the clairvoyant perception of future events. To this puzzling and fascinating aspect of psi I shall devote the next chapter.

REFERENCES

1. Flew, Antony: *A New Approach to Psychical Research.* London, 1953.
2. Kant, Immanuel: *Dreams of a Spirit-Seer.* London, 1900.
3. Ibid.
4. See *Journ. SPR, 24*: No. 450.
5. *Encyclopaedia Britannica.*
6. James, William: A case of clairvoyance, *Proc. ASPR, 1*: Part 11.
7. Buchanan, J. Rodes: The science of psychometry, *Psychical Review, 1*: No. 2, 1892.
8. See Drever, James: *A Dictionary of Psychology.* London, 1952.

Chapter 4

PRECOGNITION

> *"Premonition or precognition leads us to still more mysterious regions, where stands, half-emerging from an intolerable darkness, the gravest problem that can thrill mankind, the knowledge of the future . . .*
> *It would seem as though coming events, gathered in front of our lives, bear with crushing weight upon the uncertain and deceptive dike of the present, which is no longer able to contain them. They ooze through, they seek a crevice by which to reach us."*
>
> MAURICE MAETERLINCK

SEEMINGLY upsetting all rational notions of causal relationships beween events, precognition, the extra-sensory perception of future events, is, above all, the form of psi at which the sceptic, not unreasonably, looks askance. Of its existence, however, there can be little real doubt, for although comparatively rare it is the easiest form of psi to demonstrate with something approaching certainty, that is, to the virtual exclusion of all other explanations. If a person has a premonition, a presentiment, a prophetic dream or a prevision of some improbable occurrence, and informs others of the fact before its fulfillment, the strength of the evidence of precognition is directly related to the improbability of the occurrence.

Precognition may be in any of the forms taken by other types of clairvoyance, the most common, probably, being that of the prophetic dream. Such dreams are often of a symbolic nature, and like "normal" dreams, require interpretation. They often have the character of a warning to the percipient concerning himself or his immediate associates, but sometimes concern matters with which he has no direct connection. The literature of all civilizations abounds with stories illustrating many forms of precognition, some relating to trivial experiences, others to world-shaking events. Most are in the comparatively near future, but there are well-attested cases of predictions being fulfilled in detail many years after they were made. I have chosen the following representative examples from the more reliable accounts recorded since organized psychical research began—roughly the last hundred years.

My first case, which illustrates some of the peculiarities and distortions common to many cases of precognition, was recorded by the distinguished French researcher Joseph Maxwell. A sensitive with whom he once sat saw in her crystal a large ship, the name of which she gave as *Leutschland*. It was flying a red, white and black flag. As the vessel was steaming along in mid-ocean it suddenly became enveloped in smoke, passengers and crew rushed on to the upper deck, and the ship sank.

Eight days afterward, during which time Maxwell had told a number of people of his experience, the newspapers announced an accident to the steamship *Deutschland,* which burst a boiler in mid-ocean and was compelled to heave-to. Although the *Deutschland* did not sink, as the *Leutschland* of the crystal vision had done, the other incidents of the accident were just as foretold.[1]

Discussing this case, Maeterlinck comments: "The evidence of a man like Dr. Maxwell, especially when we have to do with a so-to-speak personal incident, possesses an importance on which it is needless to insist. We have here, therefore, several days beforehand, the very clear prevision of an event which, moreover, in no way concerns the percipient: a curious detail, but one which is not uncommon in these cases. The mistake in reading *Leutschland* for *Deutschland,* which would have been quite natural in real life, adds a note of probability and authenticity to the phenomenon. As for the final act, the foundering of the vessel in the place of a simple heaving to, we must see in this, as Dr. J. W. Pickering and W. A. Sadgrove suggest, 'the subconscious dramatization of a subliminal inference of the percipient.' Such dramatizations, moreover, are instinctive and almost general in this class of visions."[2]

Next, an instance of "psychometric" precognition. On July 7, 1928, Harry Price, a well-known British investigator, had a sitting in Paris with a *clairvoyante,* Mlle. Jeanne Laplace. The sitting was arranged by Professor Eugene Osty, at whose house it took place. Osty's sister-in-law took shorthand notes. At the beginning of the sitting Price took a letter at random from a packet he was carrying and handed it to the sensitive. It was from Dr. R. J. Tillyard, a distinguished entomologist, who was in Canada when he wrote it. The letter was so folded that it was quite impossible to discern any of its contents, or even to see whether it was typed, written or printed.

Holding the letter between her palms, Mlle. Laplace gave the "impressions" she received from it. These were noted in full and numbered by the stenographer. Of fifty-three such impressions, forty-two were subsequently confirmed to be correct or nearly correct. Price was able to confirm a number of them at the time, including the statements that the letter was typewritten, that the writer was a doctor and a scientist, that he was not in good health, that he was in London and had come from America. She also gave the word "rebec," presumably a near miss for Quebec, from where the letter had been sent.

She predicted that the writer would not live for many years, and that he would die through a railroad or automobile accident, asserting that "wheels or rails are bad for him." Later in the sitting she reiterated her prophecy, saying, "He will have a tragic death—congestion of the brain—will fall on railway or under car." (At the time Tillyard was forty-seven years old, and although by no means a fit man, he had just been passed by a medical board as good for many more years of activity.)

Price did not know at the time that wheels and rails were indeed "bad for" Dr. Tillyard. In 1913, he had been badly hurt in a railway accident in Australia, suffering concussion, a fractured arm and severe back injuries. Several years afterwards he had broken an arm again in an automobile smash in New Zealand, and later fractured a rib in another car accident, this time in America.

On January 12, 1937, near Goulburn, New South Wales, Australia, Dr. Tillyard was driving with his daughter and a friend when his car skidded and overturned, forcing his head through the windscreen and causing concussion and paralysis. He died in hospital the next day. The *clairvoyante's* prediction had been fulfilled to the letter.

The authentication of this case was virtually perfect, for Price wrote a full report of the sitting immediately afterwards, and this was published in the same year in the *Journal of the American Society for Psychical Research*.[3] Price comments, "A feature of this case is that throughout the sitting (as Mlle. Laplace afterwards admitted) the medium was obsessed with the feeling of danger from wheels or travelling on wheels. It is quite certain that she somehow sensed Tillyard's various accidents."[4]

No single event, probably, has had so many well-attested paranormal experiences related to it as the sinking of the liner *Titanic* in 1912. In a recent paper Dr. Ian Stevenson, of Virginia University, has reviewed and analyzed these experiences and has shown that a number of them were striking examples of various forms of precognition.[5]

At that time the largest vessel in the world, the White Star liner *Titanic* sailed from Southampton on her maiden voyage to New York on April 10, 1912. Of an advanced design which included such features as a double bottom and a system of watertight bulkheads, she was, so her builders claimed, unsinkable. Shortly before midnight on April 14, while steaming at full speed, she struck an iceberg, and less than three hours later, foundered, with a loss of over 1,500 lives.

The general belief of the public, the liner's passengers and crew, and her officers, in the myth of unsinkability is an important factor when considering the accounts to be described, for it reduces enormously the chances of the disaster having been inferred in a rational manner from the published information concerning the vessel.

The first presentiment of the event seems to have come, albeit unrecognized as such, to a novelist, Morgan Robertson, who, fourteen years before the sinking of the *Titanic*, wrote a story whose theme was the construction, sailing and sinking of a huge steamship called *Titan*. Like the *Titanic*, Robertson's fictional liner was considered unsinkable, but foundered after colliding with an iceberg. Stevenson sets out the remarkable similarities between the fictional vessel and real one thus:

	Titan	*Titanic*
Number of persons aboard	3,000	2,207
Number of lifeboats	24	20
Speed at impact with iceberg	25 knots	23 knots
Displacement tonnage of the liner	75,000	66,000
Length of the liner	800 feet	882.5 feet
Number of propellers	3	3

Stevenson considers the correspondence either exact or impressive on the following ten points: name of the ship; myth of unsinkability; collision with iceberg; sinking in the month of April; displacement tonnage; length of ship; speed of ship at moment of impact; number of propellers; number of lifeboats; enormous loss of life. When it is remembered that at the time when Robertson wrote his story a ship of the size and speed he envisaged would not have been thought possible, these similarities seem even more remarkable.[6]

Ten days before the *Titanic* sailed, a Mr. J. Connon Middleton, who had booked a passage in the liner, had a dream in which he seemed to see the *Titanic* "floating on the sea, keel upwards and her passengers and crew swimming around her." He seemed, he said, to be "floating in the air just above the wreck." This dream was repeated the following night. Four days after his first dream Middleton cancelled his passage (although not on account of the dreams), and told several people about them. These people subsequently testified that he had done so, his wife adding that he "never dreams," and had certainly never had a similar experience.

Among the thousands who watched the *Titanic* slip down the Solent at the beginning of her maiden, and only, voyage, were a Mrs. Marshall and her family whose house overlooked that historic strip of water. Her daughter, Joan Grant the writer, has described how, as the great liner passed, Mrs. Marshall became agitated and upset, grasped her husband's arm and cried, "That ship is going to sink before she reaches America." When her husband and other members of her family tried to reassure her by describing the features of the liner's design that rendered it "unsinkable," Mrs. Marshall became even more upset and cried, "Don't stand there staring at me! Do something! You fools, I can see hundreds of people struggling in the icy water! Are you all so blind that you are going to let them drown?" Joan Grant continues, "During the next five days, everyone was careful not to mention the *Titanic*, but Mother was nervy and Father looked harassed. It must have been almost a relief for her when everyone knew that the *Titanic* had struck an iceberg; not nearly so lonely as waiting until it happened."[7]

Several "mediums" also made predictions which seem applicable to the *Titanic* disaster, although that vessel was not specifically mentioned. On April 10, a well known British medium, Vincent Newton Turvey, forecast that "a great liner will be lost." He included this prediction in a letter to a Madame de Steiger written on April 13, adding that this would occur within two days. This letter, which was in the post at the time of the sinking, was received by Madame de Steiger on April 15, the day following the collision.[8]

W. T. Stead, well known as a journalist—he was founder and editor of the *Review of Reviews*—and a leading spiritualist, who was lost in the *Titanic,* received several forewarnings of his end through mediums, in particular W. de Kerlor and Count Hamon. He seems also to have experienced some direct foreboding of his fate for many years before he died, for shipwrecks and drownings were frequently the theme of stories and articles by him.

The earliest of these, in the *Paul Mall Gazette* in 1885, took the form of a fictional survivor's account of the sinking of a great liner, in which the majority of the passengers were described as being "doomed beforehand." A footnote to this account read: "This is exactly what might take place, and what will take place, if liners are sent to sea short of boats." (The subsequent inquiry into the sinking of the *Titanic* established that an insufficiency of lifeboats was the prime cause of the appalling loss of life in that disaster, and it was as a direct result that new maritime life-saving regulations were introduced.)

In 1892, Stead contributed a story to the *Review of Reviews* called "From the Old World to the New," the theme of which was the sinking of a great liner through collision with an iceberg and the rescue of the only survivor by the White Star liner Majestic. The master of the *Majestic,* a real liner of that time, was Captain Smith, who was later to take command of the *Titanic* and lose his life in her.

Speaking at the Cosmos Club in London in 1909, Stead, who was protesting against what he believed to be the over-rigorous attitude of the SPR in regard to alleged communications from the dead, pictured himself as ship-wrecked, drowning, and calling frantically for help. On another occasion he said that a "vision" he had experienced had convinced him that "I shall not die in a way common to the most of us, but by violence, and one of many in a throng."

In 1911, Stead was told by a medium, Count Louis Hamon (the famous "Cheiro"), that danger to his life would be from water, and from nothing else. Later in the same year the medium wrote to Stead saying that travel would be dangerous to him in the month of April, 1912.

In the same year another medium, W. de Kerlor, with whom Stead had several sittings, made a number of similar statements. On one occasion he said, "I can see . . . the picture of a huge black ship, of which I see the back portion; where the name of the ship should be written there is a wreath of immortelles. . . . I can only see half of the ship; that symbol may mean by the time this ship will be completed—when one will be able to see it in its whole length, it is perhaps then that you will go on your journey." (Kerlor had previously forecast that Stead would make a journey to America.)

Later the medium told Stead of a dream applying to him, in which he had dreamt "that I was in the midst of a catastrophe on the water; there were masses (more than a thousand) of bodies struggling in the water and I was among them. I could hear their cries for help." He also said that the black ship of which he had spoken previously "meant limitations, difficulties and death."

Many other interesting, if less evidential, experiences have also been noted in Dr. Stevenson's paper. Shortly before the *Titanic* struck the iceberg, one of her passengers, Mr. Charles M. Hays, President of the Grand Trunk Railroad, asserted that the time would soon come for "the greatest and most appalling of all disasters at sea." Major Butt, military *aide* to President Taft, wrote to his sister-in-law on February 23, 1912, telling her that he was going to Europe and saying, "Don't forget that all my papers are in the storage warehouse, and if the old ship goes down you will find my affairs in shipshape condition." He did not know then that he would be returning by the *Titanic,* in which he was lost.

It is not necessary, I am sure, to stress the need for caution in accepting the stuff of dreams and the statements of "sensitives" as accurate or even genuine predictions, although some of our most eminent researchers have, in the past, lapsed in this fashion. Myers, for instance, accepted the statement, made in 1900, of a medium in whom he had great confidence that he (Myers) would die in February, 1902, and planned the completion of his *Human Personality* on a month-by-month basis accordingly. In fact, he died in January, 1901, leaving his book unfinished. Richard Hodgson was also misled as to his expectation of life in a similar way.

The overwhelming majority of predictions are not, of course, borne out by subsequent occurrences. Hardly any precise forecasts of important events connected with the two World Wars, for instance, have been recorded, although—particularly in the case of the Second World War—numerous mediums, clairvoyants, fortunetellers, astrologers, etc., were reported as declaring that it would be averted. Of the few notable exceptions, the most striking was that concerning the Second World War made nearly thirty years before its outbreak by a noted past president of the SPR and a gifted automatist (automatic writer), Dame Edith Lyttelton.

On January 31, 1915, Dame Edith (or a discarnate entity purporting to communicate through her) wrote, "The Nemesis of Fate nearer and nearer, no respite now, nearer much than you think. . . . The Munich bond remember that." On May 24 of the same year she wrote, "The hand stretched out to stay Berchtesgaden."[9] Commenting on these "scripts," George Zorab, a famous Dutch parapsychologist who has made a special study of precognition, says, "Now that the Second World War has passed into history, we can say that the whole complex of this war could hardly have been better summed up than by the words *Munich Bond* (actually the beginning of the whole trouble), and *Berchtesgaden* (the symbol of Hitlerism—its stronghold—and Nazism). An indication on which side victory would finally be is probably given in the words, "The hand stretched out to stay. . . .!"[10]

Zorab, a former secretary of the Netherlands Society for Psychical Research and director of the European Research Centre of the Parapsychology Foundation, New York, was, I believe, the first to report the following case of precognitive dreams.

In 1900, a lady residing in Rotterdam, Holland, began to experience repeated dreams in which she seemed to see that city in ruins. Only small portions (but enough for identification) of certain buildings and streets seemed to remain, the rest having been reduced to a greyish-white stretch of level ground. From a position in the center of the city, where she seemed to stand in her dreams, a river that flows through Rotterdam was clearly visible, although at the time the intervening buildings normally rendered this impossible. Many more details were also given.

This dream, of which many people were informed, persisted with increasing frequency until the attack on Holland, in 1940, by the Germans, and the almost complete destruction by fire of the center of Rotterdam. After the rubble and debris had been cleared away, the city appeared in many details, particularly the greyish-white stretch of ground and the view of the river, almost exactly as the dreamer had first seen it more than forty years before.[11]

Another well-authenticated case of dream precognition, also from Holland, is attested by Professor W. H. C. Tenhaeff, a noted psychiatrist and now Professor of Parapsychology at the University of Utrecht. The percipient was a patient of his, a woman of forty who had been asked by Professor Tenhaeff to note any dreams that particularly impressed her and post them to his address. On November 27, 1937, Professor Tenhaeff received a letter from her, bearing that day's postmark. It contained a detailed description of a dream in which two cars had collided and one of the drivers killed. She recognized the dead man, whom she saw lying on the ground, as Prince Bernhard, consort to Queen Juliana of Holland.

Three days after the dream, in the early hours of November 29, Prince Bernhard, driving his sports car, collided with another vehicle and was thrown out, unconscious. He did not, however, die.

The circumstances of the accident were almost identical with those of the woman's dream, and her letter accurately described the spot where it took place—a railway viaduct on a long, straight stretch of road surrounded by meadows—and the types of vehicle involved. Prince Bernhard lay for some time unconscious, and with every appearance of being dead, before he was recognized by his rescuers. Of the specific items in the dream, numbering eleven, eight were completely correct, one (the apparent death of the prince) partly correct and only two definitely wrong.

Of this case Zorab comments, "Analyzing the dream a doubt may be raised whether the expression 'he was killed on the spot,' to be found in the letter, was part of the dream content. It may have been inferred from seeing the prince lying on the ground (and presumably motionless) when Mrs. O. awoke from her dream. However this may be, so many specific points of detail were mentioned that the idea of a coincidence without a real relationship between dream and future event may be dismissed as highly improbable." [12]

The best known reports of precognitive dreams, however, are undoubtedly those experienced by J. W. Dunne and described in his famous book *An Experiment with Time*.[13] Dunne, a well-known aeronautical engineer, had experienced striking dream precognitions from early childhood, many of them concerning quite trivial events, but some related to momentous happenings. In consequence he began recording his dreams daily, writing them down immediately on awakening, and later checking them for precognitive material. In this way Dunne claimed to have demonstrated that such dreams occur frequently, and that this could be verified by anyone who cared to repeat his methods. On the results of these experiments he based a complicated theory which he termed *Serialism*, in which he not only considers time to be a fourth dimension but postulates an infinite series of dimensions in time itself.

The fallaciousness of Dunne's theory has been ably and, I think, conclusively demonstrated, particularly by Professors Broad[14] and Flew.[15] Dunne's claims that precognitive dreams are common does not seem to be confirmed by most of those who have repeated his experiment. It would also appear to be refuted by what Flew terms "a powerful argument from silence, in that none of the considerable number of Dunne's readers who must have tried, however half-heartedly, to repeat his tests, seems to have got results sufficiently striking to publish."[16] One notable exception, however, is the recent work of Dr. Kooy, a leading Dutch physicist and mathematician, who has not only repeated Dunne's experiment with some success but also taken the precaution (strangely ignored by Dunne) of sending his notes immediately to an independent witness, thus establishing a proper control. These measures, according to Zorab, "made it possible to prove beyond a doubt that Kooy in his dreams received in a fragmentary manner impressions referring to future events, etc., in which he or other persons were going to participate." Kooy's dream material, Zorab adds, "as is often the case, was of a personal and emotional character and linked up with his neurotic complexes."[17]

Of the methods of testing precognitive faculties, perhaps the most elegant are the "empty chair" experiments originally devised by Professor Osty at the Institut Métapsychique, Paris, as a test of the sensitive Pascal Forthuny. Some hours before the commencement of a sitting, at which any number of persons up to about 200 might be present, an empty chair in the auditorium would be chosen at random and the sensitive asked to give his impression of the person who would later occupy it. After the audience had taken their seats, also at random, Forthuny would stand in front of the selected chair again and read out his prediction (which had been taken down at the time he made it). He was frequently successful in this manner in giving accurate descriptions of the character, state of health, profession, interests and past career of the sitter, together with forecasts of future events concerning that person.[18]

Similar "empty chair" experiments have recently been made, in many countries in Europe, with a Dutch clairvoyant, Gerard Croiset, whose successes were even more striking than those of Forthuny. Many of these experiments were organized by Professor Tenhaeff at the parapsychology laboratory of the University of Utrecht, and any information given was immediately checked by Tenhaeff. Croiset spoke his impressions concerning the future occupant of a given chair into a tape-recorder several hours, and sometimes even days, before the actual sitting took place. When Croiset could give no impressions it was usually found that the chair in question subsequently remained unoccupied. An analysis of some experiments conducted by Zorab showed that only ten to fifteen per cent of Croiset's impressions were incorrect. The descriptions were never of a vague or general nature, but "detailed, personal and very much to the point."[19]

REFERENCES

1. Maxwell, Joseph: *Metapsychical Phenomena.* London, 1905.
2. Maeterlinck, Maurice: *The Unknown Guest.* London, 1914.
3. Price, Harry: *Fifty Years of Psychical Research.* London, 1939.
4. Ibid.
5. Stevenson, Ian: A review and analysis of paranormal experiences connected with the sinking of the Titanic, *Journ. ASPR, 54*: No. 4.
6. Robertson, M.: The wreck of the Titan, *McClure's Magazine,* New York, 1898.
7. Grant, Joan: *Time Out of Mind.* London, 1956.
8. See *Light,* June, 1912.
9. See *Proc. SPR, 38*:335.
10. Zorab, George: Precognition in Holland, *Light,* December, 1957.
11. Ibid.
12. Ibid.
13. Dunne, John William: *An Experiment with Time.* London, 1927.
14. Broad, C. D.: Mr. Dunne's theory of time, *Philosophy, 10*: No. 38.
15. Flew, Antony: *A New Approach to Psychical Research.* London, 1953.
16. Ibid.
17. Zorab, George: Precognition in Holland, *Light,* December, 1957.
18. Osty, Eugene: *Une facilite de connaissance supranormale.* Paris, 1926.
19. Bender, Hans: Precognition in the qualitative experiments, Paper 38, *First International Conference of Parapsychological Studies,* Utrecht, 1953.

Chapter 5

SPIRITUALISM, SPIRITS AND MEDIUMS

*"Spiritualism is, at its best, a religion;
at its worst, a 'racket.'"*

HARRY PRICE

A MAJOR PART of the work of the early researchers was the investigation of "the various physical phenomena commonly called spiritualistic; with an attempt to discover their causes and general laws,"[1] and of the "mediums" through whom such phenomena were alleged to occur.

Perhaps the most important pioneer research of this nature was that made by a number of different investigators into the remarkable manifestations attributed to the most famous of all mediums, Daniel Dunglas Home. The career of Home (pronounced "Hume") is notable, not only for the wide variety and sensational character of the phenomena he is reported to have produced, but also because he was one of the very few "physical" mediums against whom no allegation of fraud seems ever to have been substantiated.

Born at Currie, near Edinburgh, Home claimed that his father, William Humes, was a "natural" son of Alexander, tenth Earl of Home, the change in spelling having resulted from a family quarrel. Home was adopted by an aunt with whom he went to America at the age of nine. He was a nervous, delicate child: indeed, his health was so poor that he was not expected to live.

It is said that his mother's family was well known to possess the gift of "second sight," and that Home had his first psychic experience at the age of thirteen, when he saw a "vision" of a schoolboy friend who had recently died, and with whom he had made a pact that whoever died first would attempt to appear to the other. His second experience appears to have been four years later, when he made an accurate prediction, to the exact time, of his mother's death. Shortly afterwards he began to hear loud and persistent raps which his aunt, a strictly religious woman, pronounced to be the work of the Devil, and accordingly threw him out of the house.

He went to stay with a friend, and it is remarkable that from then on, Home seems to have lived on the hospitality of his many friends and admirers. It is important to note that, so far as we know, he never accepted a penny from anyone in direct payment for his work as a medium. There is no doubt, however, that indirectly he received a great deal by way of gifts. Although he insisted that he was never a professional medium and jealously guarded his "amateur" status, Home has made it clear that this was not a question of principle, and he once wrote: "When the Archbishops of Canterbury and York return to the primitive practice of St. Peter and St. Paul, and live by catching fish and mending nets, it will be time enough to raise an outcry against mediums."[2]

Home returned to England in 1855, after causing something of a sensation in America where a number of famous men, including Professors Hare, Mapes and Wells and Judge Edmonds, testified to the reality of a wide range of phenomena—raps, tables turning, the levitation of heavy objects, the production of "spirit" lights, materialized hands that rang bells, tied knots in handkerchiefs and played musical instruments: all freely interspersed with "communications" from the "spirit world." His reputation had preceded him, and he was soon besieged by would-be witnesses of the incredible phenomena he was alleged to produce. His performances in England were, it seems, no less successful, and within a very short time a "press war" was raging between eminent men as to the genuineness or otherwise of his phenomena.

Later in the same year, Home went to the Continent and, shortly afterwards, the "spirits" told him that his psychic powers would leave him for a time. He then became a convert to Roman Catholicism and was received by the Pope. A year later, his powers returned, apparently stronger than ever, and a highly successful and colorful tour of the Continent ensued, during which he was called upon to demonstrate his gifts to many European monarchs. He married a Russian noblewoman, and after the birth of a son, returned with them to England. His wife died in 1862, and later the same year his autobiography, *Incidents in My Life,* was published.

Home made a short trip to America and then to the Continent again, and it was soon after his return to England that the only really dubious event in his life occurred. Mrs. Jane Lyon, a wealthy widow with strong spiritualistic beliefs, took a liking to Home and said that if he would alter his name to Home-Lyon she would adopt him as her son and settle £60,000 upon him. Home agreed, and received the money. Mrs. Lyon also made a will in his favor. Later she had a change of heart and sued him for the return of the money, claiming that she had been induced to make the gift by alleged spirit messages received through Home from her dead husband. Although Mrs. Lyon was largely discredited in court, the judge referring to her evidence as containing "mis-statements so perversely untrue that they have embarrassed the court to a great degree," Home lost his case, mainly on account of the prejudice against both him and "spiritualism."

In 1867-9, Home gave a number of dramatic demonstrations of his powers to Lord Adare, later to become the Earl of Dunraven, and these were recorded by the latter in a book published in 1870 entitled *Experiences in Spiritualism with Mr. D. D. Home*. In addition to reports of many phenomena of the kinds already mentioned, this book contains Adare's famous description of how Home floated out of a fourth floor window and in through that of an adjoining room. The account, which was corroborated by Lord Lindsay and Captain Charles Wynne, includes the following statements:

"We heard Home go into the next room, heard the window thrown up, and presently Home appeared standing upright outside our window; he opened the window and walked in quite coolly . . . I got up and shut the window in the next room and on coming back remarked that the window was not raised a foot, and that I could not think how he had managed to squeeze through. He arose and said 'Come and see.' I went with him: he told me to open the window as it was before. I did so: he told me to stand a little distance off; he then went through the open space, head first, quite rapidly, his body being nearly horizontal and apparently rigid. He came in again, feet foremost; and we returned to the other room . . . When Home awoke, he was much agitated, he said he felt as

The windows of the house at Victoria, London, between which the medium
D. D. Home is said to have floated. (Photograph by the author.)

The author demonstrating the accordion used by Sir William Crookes in his experiments with the medium D. D. Home. (Courtesy Society for Psychical Research, London.)

if he had gone through some fearful peril, and that he had felt a most horrible desire to throw himself out of the window."

Lord Lindsay's account includes:

"We heard the window in the next room lifted up, and almost immediately afterwards we saw Home floating in the air outside our window.

"The moon was shining full into the room. My back was to the light; and I saw the shadow on the wall of the window-sill, and

Home's feet about six inches above it. He remained in this position for a few seconds, then raised the window and glided into the room feet foremost, and sat down.

"Lord Adare then went into the next room to look at the window from which he had been carried. It was raised about eighteen inches, and he expressed his wonder how Mr. Home had been taken through so narrow an aperture.

"Home said (still in trance) 'I will show you'; and then, with his back to the window, he leaned back and was shot out of the aperture head first, with the body rigid, and then returned quite quietly.

"The window is about seventy feet from the ground. I very much doubt whether any skillful rope-dancer would like to attempt a feat of this description, where the only means of crossing would be a perilous leap.

"The distance between the windows was about seven feet six inches, and there was not more than a twelve-inch projection to each window, which served as a ledge to put flowers on."

Much controversy has centered around these reports, about which, alas, it seems unlikely that any decisive conclusions will ever now be reached.

We come now to what is, to the psychical researcher at least, a particularly interesting phase of Home's career. In 1871 the famous physicist and chemist William Crookes, F.R.S., who was later to receive a knighthood in recognition of his scientific work, announced the result of a series of experiments he had conducted in which Home was subjected to many exacting tests. The introduction to his report contained the following statement:

"Among the most remarkable phenomena which occur under Mr. Home's influence, the most striking, as well as the most easily tested with scientific accuracy, are (1) the alteration in the weight of bodies and (2) the playing of tunes upon musical instruments (generally an accordion, for convenience of portability) without direct human intervention, under conditions rendering contact or connection with the keys an impossibility. Not until I had witnessed these facts some half-dozen times, and scrutinized them with all the critical acumen I possess, did I become convinced of their objective reality. Still, desiring to place the matter beyond the shadow of doubt, I invited Mr. Home to come to my own house, where, in the presence of a few scientific enquirers, these phenomena could be submitted to crucial experiments."[3]

To Crookes belongs the distinction of being the first to make extensive use of scientific apparatus in psychical research, and the equipment he used in the investigation of Home included, in addition to a number of electrical devices he designed himself, instruments for recording variations of temperature and weight and an accordion in a "cage" constructed of insulated copper wire. In spite of his scientific approach, however, Crookes was unable to induce any members of the leading scientifc societies to witness his experiments, and he confessed to being "surprised and pained at the timidity or apathy shown by scientific men in reference to this subject."

To the astonishment of the scientific world, Crookes's report confirmed that the amazing phenomena attributed to Home were facts, seeming to indicate the existence of "a new force, in some unknown manner connected with the human organization, which for convenience may be called the Psychic Force."

Crookes divided the phenomena he claimed to have observed into thirteen different classes.

1. *The Movement of Heavy Bodies with Contact, but without Mechanical Exertion.* This Crookes considered one of the simplest forms of psychic phenomena. It varied in degree "from a quivering or vibration of the room and its contents to the actual rising into the air of a heavy body when the hand is placed on it."

2. *The Phenomena of Percussive and other Allied Sounds.* These included the familiar "raps" and appeared to be governed by intelligence. "At a very early stage of the inquiry it was seen that the power producing the phenomena was not merely a blind force, but was associated with or governed by intelligence: thus the sounds . . . will be repeated a definite number of times, they will come loud or faint, and in different places at request, and by a prearranged code of signals, questions are answered and messages given with more or less accuracy."

3. *The Alteration of Weight of Bodies.* Crookes claimed that

with his apparatus he had measured substantial changes in weight.

4. *Movements of Heavy Substances when at a Distance from the Medium.* Crookes stated: "The instances in which heavy bodies, such as tables, chairs, sofas, etc., have been moved, when the medium has not been touching them, are very numerous . . . My own chair has been twisted partly round, whilst my feet were off the floor. A chair was seen by all present to move slowly up to a table from a far corner when all were watching it; on another occasion an armchair moved to where we were sitting and then moved slowly back again (a distance of about three feet) at my request. On three successive evenings a small table moved slowly across the room, under conditions which I had specially pre-arranged, so as to answer any objection which might be raised to the evidence."

5. *The Rising of Tables and Chairs off the Ground, without Contact with any Person.* "On five separate occasions a heavy dining-table rose between a few inches and one and one-half feet off the floor, under special circumstances which rendered trickery impossible. On another occasion a heavy table rose from the floor in full light, while I was holding the medium's hands and feet. On another occasion the table rose from the floor, not only when no person was touching it, but under conditions which I had pre-arranged so as to ensure unquestionable proof of the fact."

6. *The Levitation of Human Beings.* Crookes claimed that on three separate occasions he had seen Home raised completely from the floor—once sitting in an easy chair, once kneeling on his chair and once standing up.

7. *Movement of Various Small Articles without Contact with Any Person.* Here Crookes comments: " . . . what I relate has not been accomplished at the house of a medium, but in my own house, where preparations have been quite impossible. A medium, walking into my dining-room, cannot, while seated in one part of the room with a number of persons keenly watching him, by trick-ery make an accordion play in *my own* hand when I hold it keys downwards, or cause the same accordion to float about the room playing all the time. He cannot introduce machinery which will wave window-curtains, or pull up Venetian blinds eight feet off,

tie a knot in a handkerchief and place it in a far distant corner of the room, sound notes on a distant piano, cause a card-plate to float about the room, raise a water-bottle and tumbler from the table, make a coral necklace rise on end, cause a fan to move about and fan the company, or set in motion a pendulum when enclosed in a glass case firmly cemented to the wall."

8. *Luminous Appearances*. Crookes affirmed that under the strictest test conditions he had observed a self-luminous body, similar in size and shape to a turkey's egg, float about the room at a height greater than could be reached by anyone present: he had seen points of light darting about and settling on the heads of different persons: had questions answered by flashing lights and *"in the light* [I have] seen a luminous cloud hover over a heliotrope on a side table, break a sprig off and carry the sprig to a lady; and on some occasions I have seen a similar luminous cloud visibly condense to the form of a hand and carry small objects about."

9. *The Appearance of Hands, either Self-Luminous or Visible by Ordinary Light*. Crookes claimed to have *felt* such hands frequently at "dark seances," and on rare occasions to have seen them. He noted especially the following four instances.

"A beautifully formed small hand rose up from an opening in a dining-table and gave me a flower; it appeared and then disappeared three times at intervals, affording me ample opportunity of satisfying myself that it was as real in appearance as my own. This occurred in the light in my own room, whilst I was holding the medium's hands and feet.

"On another occasion a small hand and arm, like a baby's, appeared playing about a lady who was sitting next to me. It then passed to me and patted my arm and pulled my coat several times.

"At another time a finger and thumb were seen to pick the petals from a flower in Mr. Home's buttonhole and lay them in front of several persons who were sitting near him.

"A hand has repeatedly been seen by myself and others playing the keys of an accordion, both of the medium's hands being visible at the same time, and sometimes being held by those near him."

According to Crookes the hands sometimes appeared "icy cold and dead," at other times warm and lifelike, "grasping my own with the firm pressure of an old friend." When he attempted to hold one of these hands and prevent it from escaping no struggle or effort was made to get loose, the hand seeming to "resolve into vapor" and thus fade from his grasp.

10. *Direct Writing.* Crookes reported witnessing this class of phenomena both with Home and with another medium, Kate Fox, and asserted that he had seen a luminous hand descend, take a pencil from his hand, write rapidly on a sheet of paper, throw the pencil down and then rise up over the heads of the sitters, gradually fading into darkness. He also reported seeing a pencil stand on end by itself in good light and after making a few jerks forward attempt, unsuccessfully, to write.

11. *Phantom Forms and Faces.* This class, also known as materialization, Crookes regarded as the rarest type of phenomena, and admitted to observing satisfactory examples only on a very few occasions. He recorded the two following examples as among the best he had witnessed:

. "In the dusk of the evening, during a seance with Mr. Home at my house, the curtains of the window about eight feet from Mr. Home were seen to move. A dark, shadowy, semi-transparent form, like that of a man, was then seen by all present, standing near the window, waving the curtain with his hand. As we looked the form faded away and the curtains ceased to move.

"As in the former case, Mr. Home was the medium. A phantom form came from a corner of the room, took an accordion in its hand, and then glided about the room playing the instrument. The form was visible to all present for many minutes, Mr. Home also being seen at the same time. Coming rather close to a lady who was sitting apart from the rest of the company, she gave a slight cry, upon which it vanished."

12. *Special Instances which seem to point to the Agency of an Exterior Intelligence.* Under this heading Crookes gave examples of automatic writing, planchette operation and "rapping," in which information believed to be unknown to the medium or to any of the sitters was given.

13. *Miscellaneous Occurrences of a Complex Character.* Here Crookes grouped a number of phenomena which he could not

otherwise classify owing to their complex character. Most of these were examples of *apports*—articles transported from other rooms, etc., which appeared to indicate that matter had passed through matter. The most extraordinary of these was when a luminous appearance was seen over a vase of flowers which stood on the table of the seance-room, and then "in full view of all present, a piece of china-grass fifteen inches long, which formed the center ornament of the bouquet, slowly rose from the other flowers, and then descended to the table in front of the vase between it and Mr. Home. It did not stop on reaching the table, but went straight through it, and we all watched it till it had entirely passed through. Immediately on the disappearance of the grass my wife, who was sitting near Mr. Home, saw a hand come up from under the table between them, holding the piece of grass. It tapped her on the shoulder two or three times with a sound audible to all, then laid the grass on the floor and disappeared."

Home did little as a medium after the Crookes experiments, and retired to Paris, where he died at the age of fifty-three in 1886. Of him, the Earl of Dunraven, who had also investigated his mediumship on many occasions, wrote: " . . . he was withal of a simple, kindly, humorous. lovable disposition that appealed to me. He never took money, for seances failed as often as not. He was proud of his gift but not happy in it. He could not control it and it placed him sometimes in very unpleasant positions. I think he would have been pleased to have been relieved of it, but I believe he was subject to these manifestations as long as he lived."

And Sir William Crookes said:

"During the whole of my knowledge of D. D. Home, extending for several years, I never once saw the slightest occurrence that would make me suspicious that he was attempting to play tricks. He was scrupulously sensitive on this point, and never felt hurt at anyone taking precautions against deception. To those who knew him Home was one of the most lovable of men and his perfect genuineness and uprightness were above suspicion."

Crookes is also famous as a psychical researcher for his investigation of the best known of all "materializing" mediums, Florence Cook (1856-1904), about whose alleged phenomena more controversy has raged, and still rages, than with any other medium in the history of parapsychology.

The most extraordinary of these phenomena was the production of a full-form materialization of the spirit of a young woman claiming to be "Katie King," the daughter of John King, alias the notorious pirate Henry Morgan. A sensation was caused in 1874, when Crookes announced that he had not only witnessed, but had photographed the materializations, which he pronounced genuine. He averred that he had seen the entranced medium still in the "cabinet" at the same time as the materialized spirit was walking about in the seance room, that he had carried on normal conversations with her, and even, on one occasion, embraced her.

Prior to 1962, most of the controversy over Crookes's report was on the question of whether the phenomena were genuine or Crookes had been deceived by the medium. In that year, however, valuable new light was thrown on the matter by the publication of the report of a painstaking investigation by a British researcher, Trevor H. Hall, entitled *The Spiritualists*. In the course of extensive enquiries Hall unearthed much new material, which appears to show conclusively that far from being deluded, Crookes was a leading partner in a gigantic hoax, the purpose of which was to cover up an illicit affair (one of many in which Florence had indulged) between the medium and himself. In the light of Hall's report it seems extremely doubtful that Florence Cook ever produced any genuine psychic phenomena.

One of the most celebrated and respected mediums of this period was William Stainton Moses (1839-1892), an English clergyman whose life has been described by F. W. H. Myers as "one of the most extraordinary of the nineteenth century." Moses took his M.A. (Oxon.) and was ordained in 1863, and in the following year became a curate in the Isle of Man. Ill health forced his retirement from church office seven years later, when he took a mastership at University College School, London, a post which he retained until within four years of his death.

As a schoolboy he is known to have been a somnambulist, and it is on record that he was once seen by his brother to write an excellent essay in his sleep. His first psychic experiences seem to

Two of the notebooks of the medium W. Stainton Moses. (Courtesy College of Psychic Science, London.)

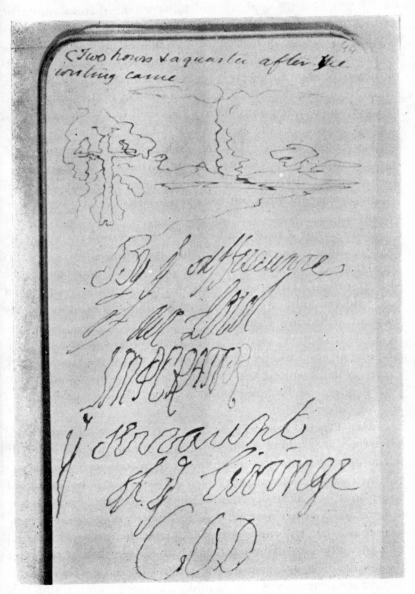

A page of one of the notebooks of W. Stainton Moses. (Courtesy College of Psychic Science, London.) .

have begun in 1872, and are said to have ranged from automatic
writing and trance speaking to levitation, the movement of heavy
objects, the passage of matter through matter and the production
of music when no instruments of any kind were around. Moses is
most widely known, however, for his prolific automatic writings,
which were alleged to emanate from a band of exalted spirits, and
many of which were published in a famous book, *Spirit Teachings*,
often described as "the spiritualists' bible." Whatever the true
source of these writings, they are remarkable for the amazing differences in calligraphy shown by the various "communicators.'
The original notebooks are now in the keeping of the College of
Psychic Science, London, and are open to inspection by any serious
inquirer.

Moses made a strong and favorable impression on a number
of the leading researchers of the time, including F. W. H. Myers
and Edmund Gurney. He was one of the first members of the
SPR, but resigned from that society in 1886 in protest against what
he considered to be an unfair official attitude towards some of the
mediums it had investigated.

The first great "mental" medium to submit to serious scientific investigation was the famous American sensitive Mrs. Leonore
Piper. Notable among the eminent researchers who studied her
psychic gifts were Professor William James, Dr. Richard Hodgson
and Sir Oliver Lodge.

Mrs. Piper is said to have had her first psychic experience
when she was a child of eight. One day, while at play, she suddenly
felt a blow on her right ear followed by a strange hissing noise.
She then seemed to hear a voice saying, "Aunt Sarah, not dead, but
with you still." Naturally frightened by such a strange occurrence,
she ran and told her mother, who fortunately had the good sense
to note the date and time. A few days later the news was received
that an aunt whose name was Sarah had, in fact, died at the exact
time of the girl's strange experience. For some time following this
occurrence Leonore was unable to sleep at night, complaining that
she saw a bright light in her room "with many faces in it." In general, however, she seems to have spent a perfectly normal childhood.

When in her early twenties, Mrs. Piper, who had recently

married, had a sitting in Boston with a medium named Cocke, during which she fell into a trance. In consequence she joined a "developing circle" under the guidance of Cocke, and soon began to see various lights and faces. On one occasion she went into a trance during which she wrote down a statement on a piece of paper, and when this was handed to another member of the circle, Judge Frost, he declared that the message was such as could only have come from one person, his deceased son.

The news of this and similar amazing achievements quickly spread, and Mrs. Piper was soon inundated with requests for sittings. Fortunately for psychical research she came to the notice of William James, who, following a number of impressive personal sittings, assumed complete control of her psychic career. This responsibility later passed to Dr. Richard Hodgson, and it was during the period of his supervision that the most impressive products of her mediumship, the famous "communications" from George Pelham, were received.

"George Pelham" was the pseudonym adopted by a friend of Hodgson, a young lawyer, who had a sitting with Mrs. Piper in 1888. She was never informed of his true identity. A month after his death four years later, messages purporting to be from him were received through Mrs. Piper. During the next six years a total of over one hundred and fifty sitters, many of whom he had known while alive, received "communications" from "Pelham" through Mrs. Piper. Of those he had known, thirty were recognized, although they were certainly not known to the medium, and on no occasion did "Pelham" claim acquaintance with a sitter he had never known. The details of his associations with his former friends, who were always introduced pseudonymously to the medium, were so accurately and realistically discussed that Hodgson was impelled to write: "Through the years the manifestations behaved like a continuous, living and persistent personality, the only observable change being not of disintegration, but rather of integration and evolution."

In most of the Pelham "communications" names were given correctly and the appropriate degree of intimacy with the sitter indicated. In one doubtful instance, "Pelham" at first failed to recognize the sitter, Miss Warner, but as he had only known her slightly as a child this seems quite natural. He was able to give perfectly correct information concerning her relatives. Of the many sitters whom he had not known during his lifetime "Pelham" showed no knowledge at all.

In marked contrast to the extravagant claims by the vast majority of mediums concerning their "guides," Mrs. Piper declared herself unconvinced that the "communications" received through her emanated from discarnate sources or that her "controls" were, in fact, the spirits of the dead which they purported to be. One of them who called himself Phinuit was obviously a "phoney," for although he claimed to be the spirit of a French doctor from Marseilles he knew but little of the French language and still less of medical terms. Attempts to verify his claims were all abortive. Another "phoney" was conjured up by an experimenter who invented a deceased niece whom he named "Bessie Beale," and requested Mrs. Piper's "control" to make contact with her spirit. Messages from the fictitious niece's "spirit" were duly "communicated."

A remarkable feature of Mrs. Piper's trances was the degree of dissociation which took place in different parts of her body. On at least one occasion, for instance, she wrote a different "message" with each hand, at the same time delivering a third "communication" orally. Some of her trance utterances and automatic writings formed part of a famous series known as the "cross-correspondences," in which the "scripts" of a number of mediums, although appearing individually meaningless, seemed, when pieced together, to indicate that purposeful intelligences were originating them. These cross-correspondences, which were carried out under the auspices of the SPR, are widely recognized as some of the strongest evidence in support of the "survival" hypothesis.

Closely resembling that of Mrs. Piper is the mediumship of a British sensitive of a later generation, Mrs. Gladys Osborne Leonard. Like Mrs. Piper, she too is famous, not only for the quality of her mediumship, but for her integrity and her willingness to submit to scientific investigation. According to her autobiography[4] Mrs. Leonard's mediumship dates from her early childhood, when she was constantly seeing "visions." As a young woman she took part in some "table-turning" experiments, in the course of which her "control"—purportedly the spirit of a young Indian girl named Feda who had died in the year 1800—first "came through."

Shortly before the first World War, Mrs. Leonard was instructed by "Feda" to become a professional medium, with the prophecy that "something big and terrible is going to happen to the world, and Feda must help many people through you." ("Feda" always spoke in the third person.) After the death on active service of his son, Sir Oliver Lodge had many sittings with Mrs. Leonard, and as a result became convinced that he had received evidence of his son's post-mortem existence. Upon publication of his book *Raymond* which contained accounts of these sittings, Mrs. Leonard became, almost literally, famous overnight.

After the war, Mrs. Leonard gave many sittings to leading members of the SPR, notably the Reverend C. Drayton Thomas, who contributed numerous reports on her mediumship to the SPR *Journal* and *Proceedings*. Thomas evolved the technique of "book tests," which were designed to exclude the possibility of telepathy between sitter and medium. In such tests, the medium or the purporting communicator, refers to a book in the sitter's or some other library, possibly describing the position in which it will be found, and indicating the page upon which relevant information appears.

Similar tests were made with newspapers and in these, the "communicator," allegedly the spirit of Thomas's father, frequently gave evidence of a remarkable precognitive quality by forecasting items which were to appear in a national newspaper on a day subsequent to the sitting concerned.

Drayton Thomas made the notes of his sittings with Mrs. Leonard available to W. Whately Carington when the latter carried out his noted quantitative study of mediumship, and collaborated closely with him in this work, although he disagreed strongly with Carington's conclusion that "Feda" was not a spirit entity, but merely a secondary personality of the medium. Carington's view, however, received formidable support from the results of his application of the psychological technique known as the word-association test, which he made on Mrs. Leonard and a number of other trance mediums.

This test was first applied to a medium in her normal state of consciousness, and then, with the medium in trance, to her "control" or "guide." In most cases, and certainly in that of Mrs. Leonard, it was found that stimulus-words to which the medium herself responded quickly evoked exceptionally long reaction times when given to the "control" and *vice versa,* indicating that the "control" was not a personality separate and distinct from the medium, but rather a secondary personality built up from material suppressed during the medium's normal waking life.[5]

Unlike Mrs. Piper, who was never convinced that the messages received through her were from discarnate spirits, Mrs. Leonard firmly believes that she acts as a link between this world and the next, and this view is held about themselves by the vast majority of mediums. A notable exception, however, is the last of the mediums to whom I shall refer in this chapter, Eileen J. Garrett, regarded by many as the world's greatest living sensitive.

Mrs. Garrett is, I would say, without doubt the most versatile and colorful figure in psychical research today, for in addition to her fame as a medium she has earned universal recognition as a parapsychologist in her own right. A prolific and able writer on the subject, she is the author of several books and numerous papers and articles. She was also the founder and former editor of *Tomorrow,* one of the leading journals devoted to psychical research, and is president of the Parapsychology Foundation, New York, a body whose purpose is the furtherance of this work. Her life story is recorded in her autobiography, *My Life as a Search for the Meaning of Mediumship.*

Mrs. Garrett, whose ancestry is Irish and French on her mother's side, and Spanish on that of her father, underwent a wide range of psychic experiences in early childhood, but did not commence working as a medium until the mid-1920s. Within a few years, however, she built up a reputation as an exceptional and reliable trance medium.

The most sensational demonstration of her mediumship was undoubtedly that given at her famous and widely cited "R.101" seance. Although the general circumstances are well known, the importance of this seance demands a fairly detailed account in any book intended as a comprehensive introduction to matters psychic, particularly in view of the fact that it is generally recognized to be one of the cases most difficult to explain other than by the hypothesis of spirit communication. I therefore make no apology for retreading ground I have already covered elsewhere.[6]

On the 2nd October, 1930, a well known British investigator, Harry Price,* at that time director of the "National Laboratory of Psychical Research," London, engaged Mrs. Garrett for a seance to be held on the 7th October. In the early hours of Sunday, the 5th October, the great new airship, R.101, crashed on a hillside in France with the loss of all but six of her passengers and crew. The seance took place as arranged on the following Tuesday afternoon, its object being the attempt to establish communication with the late Sir Arthur Conan Doyle.

As soon as Mrs. Garrett had gone into a trance her "control" announced that someone named Irving or Irwin was anxious to speak. The medium's voice changed, and in short, sharp phrases, as if laboring under great difficulties, announced that Flight Lieutenant Irwin, captain of the R.101, was speaking. He went on to give a detailed, accurate and highly technical account of the disaster and of the events preceding it, together with a description of the many faults of design and construction which were the cause of the crash. Among his statements were the following:

"Whole bulk of the dirigible was too much for her engine capacity." "Engines too heavy." "Useful lift too small." "Oil pipe plugged." "Load too great for long flight." "Never reached cruising altitude." "Airscrews too small." "Gross lift computed badly." "Impossible to rise." "Too short trials." "Fabric waterlogged and ship's nose down." "Severe tension on the fabric, which is chafing." "Cruising speed bad and ship swinging badly." "No one knew ship properly." "Starboard strakes started." "Elevator jammed." "Added middle section entirely wrong." "Superstructure of envelope contained no resilience and far too much weight on envelope." "This exorbitant scheme of carbon and hydrogen is entirely and absolutely wrong." "We almost scraped the roofs of Achy." "Kept to railway."

---

*Not to be confused with Professor H. H. Price, a past president of the SPR.

At the subsequent enquiry into the circumstances of the crash practically all these statements were shown to be correct, although none of those who attended the seance, and emphatically not Mrs. Garrett, had the slightest knowledge of aviation. None of the remaining statements was proved incorrect, and all may well have been true; indeed, several were shown to be probably correct. The statement concerning the roofs of Achy is of special interest, for although it is such a small village that no ordinary maps show it and it is not named in guide books, it *was* shown on the special large scale flying maps used in the navigation of the airship. Evidence was given at the inquiry that the R.101 passed over Achy at a height of not more than three hundred feet from the ground.

Concluding a personal account of this seance, Harry Price states:

"It is inconceivable that Mrs. Garrett could have acquired the R.101 information through normal channels, and the case strongly supports the hypothesis of 'Survival' . . . Telepathy between the living will not cover the facts, though some sort of nexus between the living and the dead would. No one present at the seance was consciously thinking of the R.101 disaster, and no one had any technical knowledge of airships."[7]

I must emphasize here that the mediums mentioned in this chapter are by no means typical of those generally practising in the spiritualist "movement." Indeed, mediumship of this calibre is all too rare and few, if any, other mediums of a comparable standard have appeared since modern spiritualism began. With the vast majority of mediums a wide variety of non-psychic factors is far more in evidence than any genuine paranormal ability.

Apart from deliberate fraud, and there is much of this, particularly among "materialization," "direct voice" and similar mediums who specialize in the production of "physical" phenomena, there is a great deal of "unconscious cheating," where the medium, albeit unknowingly, reacts to sensory clues and "leads" from the sitter and on facts already known to her. A good example of the latter was provided by a medium who told an SPR investigator, Mrs. K. M. Goldney, during a "demonstration of clairvoyance" that she had communications for her from two spirits, "Bessie

White" and "Alec White." Reference to her records enabled Mrs. Goldney to establish that nearly two years previously, at a private sitting with this medium, she had acknowledged acquaintance with two alleged "spirits" of these names, though they were in fact quite unknown to her.

There is also a large measure of self-delusion on the part of both mediums and sitters, heightened in many cases by varying degrees of dissociation and self-hypnosis.

Even when a medium possesses a genuine psychic faculty, the information given is so often colored by her own opinions and interspersed with stock phrases or "padding," that it becomes almost unrecognizable. This is especially noticeable at most of the "demonstrations of clairvoyance" forming a major part of spiritualist religious services, where the atmosphere is invariably tense and emotional, and many of those taking part are possessed of the "will to believe" to such a degree that any "message," however banal, is accepted as evidence that departed friends and relations continue to exist on "the other side."

This question of survival of bodily death is, alas, by no means such a simple one as the less critical type of spiritualist would have us believe. Later I shall outline some of the factors that have led many eminent psychical researchers to a belief in survival and others, no less eminent, to a diametrically opposite view.

REFERENCES

1. Objects of the Society, *Proc. SPR, 1*: Part 1.
2. Home, Daniel Dunglas: *Incidents in My Life.* London, 1872.
3. Crookes, Sir William: *Researches in the Phenomena of Spiritualism.* London, 1874.
4. Leonard, Gladys Osborne: *My Life in Two Worlds.* London, 1931.
5. Carington, W. Whately: The quantitative study of trance personalities, *Proc. SPR, 42*: Part 136, *43*: Part 141, *44*: Part 149, *45*: Part 159.
6. Edmunds, Simeon: *Hypnotism and the Supernormal.* London, 1961.
7. Price, Harry: *Fifty Years of Psychical Research.* London, 1939.

Chapter 6

THE "HIGHER PHENOMENA" OF HYPNOTISM

> *"It is evident that cryptesthesia can exist apart from the hypnotic state; but it is no less well established that hypnosis increases cryptesthesia. Various persons quite incapable of any transcendental manifestations when their senses are awake, become lucid when hypnotized."*
>
> CHARLES RICHET

MANY KINDS of phenomena associated with hypnotism—trance, catalepsy, hallucinations, the carrying out of post-hypnotic suggestions and the use of hypnosis as an anaesthetic—were once regarded as paranormal in themselves. This, of course, is no longer believed, although the true nature of such phenomena is still incompletely understood. From Mesmer onward, however, hypnotists have also from time to time repeated the claim that certain entranced subjects were able to demonstrate what the early "magnetizers" termed the "higher phenomena"—clairvoyance, thought transference, the perception of future events and the diagnosis of disease—although they were quite incapable of such feats when in a normal waking state of consciousness. Mesmerism was regarded by many of the early spiritualists as the method *par excellence* of developing psychic sensitivity, and not a few of the best known mediums of the nineteenth century began their careers as hypnotic subjects.

There seems little doubt that Mesmer himself observed such phenomena among his subjects, for in his writings we find frequent indirect allusions to them. He refers to mankind as being "gifted with a sensitivity by which he can be *en rapport* with the beings who surround him, even at a great distance." Elsewhere he states, "At times somnambulism can perceive the past and the future by means of the inner sense," and again, "Man, by his inner sense, is in touch with the whole of nature and is always capable of feeling the concatenation of cause and effect. Everything in the universe is present; past and future are only different relations of the separate parts."

The earliest record of the direct use of hypnotism to increase psychic perception seems to be that of the Marquis de Puysegur, a pupil of Mesmer, who reported that a peasant boy, normally rather stupid, when hypnotized showed not only increased intelligence but remarkable powers of clairvoyance. De Puysegur experimented with a number of different subjects and achieved similar results. He noted that sometimes another personality would seem to emerge, possessing higher faculties and clearer vision. He observed also that after the termination of hypnosis no memory of what had occurred during the trance seemed to remain.

Similar claims were made in a treatise on "artificial somnambulism" published in 1820 by a French physician, Alexandre Bertrand, who asserted that not only did certain of his subjects become clairvoyant, but that a "community of sensation" could sometimes be established between hypnotist and subject. He also found that "willed" instructions were sometimes as effective as verbal ones. At about the same time the Baron du Potet, one of the first to recognize the value of hypnotism as an anaesthetic, demonstrated "mesmerism at a distance" to the French Academy of Medicine.

In 1850, Dr. Herbert Mayo, F.R.S., Professor of Physiology at the Royal College of Surgeons, reported success in "community of sensation" experiments, claiming: "The entranced person, who has no feeling or taste or smell of his own, feels, tastes and smells everything that is made to tell on the sense of the operator. If mustard or sugar be put in his [the subject's] own mouth he seems not to know they are there; if mustard is placed on the tongue of the operator the entranced person expresses great disgust and tries to spit it out. The same with bodily pain. If you pluck a hair from the operator's head, the other complains of the pain you have given him."

Successful experiments in community of sensation were also reported by many other pioneers of hypnotism, including Elliotson, Esdaile, Gregory and Braid. Similar successes at a later period by Sir William Barrett and Edmund Gurney were important factors in the founding of the Society for Psychical Research, and much of the early work of that society was devoted to a study of the connection of hypnotism with telepathy and other forms of psi.

The most impressive of the Barrett and Gurney experiments were those involving the transference of pain from hypnotist to subject. In these tests a well-known hypnotist, G. A. Smith, took part, and stringent precautions were taken to prevent communication through the normal channels of sense. The entranced subject was blindfolded and the hypnotist stood behind him. One of the experimenters then silently pricked or punched the hypnotist in various parts of the body, the only words spoken being questions asking the subject what he felt. Out of twenty-four such tests, the exact spot in which the hypnotist had been pricked or punched was correctly indicated by the subject twenty times. Equally striking results were obtained in transference of taste experiments.

G. A. Smith was also the hypnotist in famous experiments in thought-transference carried out by Professor and Mrs. Sidgwick at Brighton in 1889, some of which were also witnessed by Sir William Barrett. Most of the tests involved the guessing of numbers taken from a bag, but the transference of mental pictures seems also to have been successful. The degree of success varied from day to day, the tests proving fruitless on one and astonishingly successful on another. Many years later the percipient in these experiments, named Blackburn, made a "confession" alleging that Smith and he were in collusion and had cheated. When he made his "confession" Blackburn was under the impression that Smith was no longer alive. He was mistaken, however, for Smith came forward with a complete denial of the allegation, which appears to have been without any foundation.

One of the earliest reports of the experimental induction of hypnosis by telepathy was made by Esdaile, who claimed to have succeeded in hypnotizing a blind man on a number of occasions by gazing steadily at him from a distance of twenty yards. To safeguard against the possibility of giving sensory impressions Esdaile used to gaze at the man over a wall, often, as he stated, "at untimely hours, when he could not possibly know of my being in his neighborhood, and always with like results."

A classic series of experiments, reported by F. W. H. Myers in 1885, was that in which a French doctor, Gibert, hypnotized a subject telepathically when she was in a house some distance away, and caused her to walk, in deep trance, through the streets of Le Havre to his house. These experiments, which were successful nineteen times out of a total of twenty-five, were witnessed not only by F. W. H. Myers, but by his brother Dr. A. T. Myers, Professor Pierre Janet, Dr. Ochorowicz, and several other investigators of the highest reputation.[1]

The same subject, "Leonie," also featured in some experiments conducted by Janet in "travelling clairvoyance," including the celebrated case in which she was sent on what Janet termed a "psychic excursion" from Le Havre to Paris to see Professor Charles Richet. On that occasion she cried out in great agitation, "It is burning! It is burning!" and Janet subsequently ascertained that Richet's laboratory was, in fact, damaged by a fire on that day.

Another class of phenomena, reported by de Rochas and others, is that usually known as "exteriorization of sensibility" in which the senses of the subject appear to be transferred to such objects as wax dolls, photographs, or even glasses of water. Thus, a subject, given a doll to hold when under hypnosis, later complained of pain in the equivalent places when the doll was pricked by a pin. Similar results under test conditions were produced in 1919 in Mexico by Dr. Pagenstecher, who had accidentally discovered an exceptional subject, Señora Reyes de Z.

Pagenstecher's subject also excelled at object-reading, or psychometry. When, hypnotized, she was given an object to hold, she was able to obtain clear impressions of places and events connected with it. A piece of Roman marble, for instance, enabled her to give a detailed and accurate description of the Forum and its temples, a description on which she enlarged by making a number of drawings. She declared that she did not merely see the events, but felt as if she were actually taking part in them. All her senses were alert, and she heard, felt, saw, tasted, and seemed to live in the scenes like one virtually present.

Señora Reyes de Z. was tested by several leading American investigators, including the noted researcher Dr. Walter Franklin Prince, with impressive results. On one occasion, Prince handed her a coat which a farmer had been wearing when he was murdered. In spite of repeated attempts, her only impression was of a cloth factory. When, however, her finger was placed on a bloodstain on the coat, she at once gave a detailed account of the circumstances of the murder. Neither Prince nor Pagenstecher had any knowledge of the manner in which the crime had been committed, but subsequent enquiries proved the subject's account to be correct.[2]

Apart from the work of Pagenstecher, little interest in hypnosis seems to have been shown by psychical researchers from the turn of the century until the end of the Second World War. Since the war ended, however, there has been a marked revival of interest in this field, and the results so far achieved by the use of modern techniques and in the light of our greater knowledge of the nature of hypnosis appear highly promising.

Credit for this resurgence of interest is largely due to a Swedish psychologist, Dr. John Bjorkhem of Stockholm, who made a vast number of hypnotic experiments involving more than three thousand subjects, many of whom appeared to possess extrasensory powers when hypnotized. An exceptional subject once described to Dr. Bjorkhem a scene in her home which was several hundred miles away. She reported the actions of her parents and even mentioned an item in a newspaper which her father was reading. Soon afterwards the parents telephoned to enquire whether anything was amiss with her. They declared that her "apparition" had appeared to them, and they feared that it meant bad news.

Of the more recent experiments in "exteriorization of sensibility" and "community of sensation," the best known are probably those by Jarl Fahler, president of the Society for Psychical Research in Finland. Fahler's experiments were largely in the form of what he terms "water glass tests," of which the following description is typical:

Fahler placed a glass of water in the hypnotized subject's hands, suggesting to her that "all sense of feeling and pain was being drained" from her into the water in the glass she was holding. It was then found that when a pin was stuck into the water the subject reacted, although there was no reaction when she herself was pricked. Care was taken, of course, to ensure that she obtained no sensory clues. The same success was attained when the glass was taken from the subject and placed on a table. Equal success resulted when Fahler, and later a third person, took the glass into another room. Variations included blowing on the water instead of pricking it, and the substitution of different objects, including an apple and another person, for the water. All were successful.

Fahler has also reported outstanding success with "travelling clairvoyance" or "psychic excursions" by the same subject. On one occasion in 1953, when asked whether a "Mr. X," whom she knew by sight but about whose private affairs she was completely ignorant, would shortly be going abroad, she replied that it depended, on many things, but that he was waited for in many parts of the world.

Questioned further, she described, in some detail, an Italian man who was waiting to see Mr. X and staying at a hotel in London. His name, she said, was Piovene, adding that she could see it printed on the corner of the paper on which he was writing. He was using a fountain pen, not writing in script but printing each letter separately. She also spoke of his agitated manner, and of seeing him drumming his fingers on the table and fidgeting with a pin. She said that although the man looked like "a good fellow" Mr. X should be cautious in his dealings with him.

Fahler subsequently checked that Mr. X did know a man named Piovene, whose appearance and habits coincided accurately with the description given by the subject. This man was waiting to see Mr. X, and on the date concerned was in fact staying at the Savoy Hotel in London. At a later date Mr. X told Fahler that he wished he had taken seriously the subject's warning concerning business dealings with Piovene, for now he had good reason to regret not having done so.[3]

It is noteworthy that Fahler's subject, like others I have mentioned previously, had the feeling that she herself was present at the scene of the events described on these "psychic excursions," and experienced a distinct feeling of "coming back into the body" afterwards. The most successful subjects in experiments I have conducted myself have also reported experiencing these feelings. One subject, "Miss B," would give a running commentary on her "movements" not only at the scene of an "excursion," but during her "travelling" to and from the place concerned.

Miss B is an extremely good subject who can be kept deeply hypnotized for long periods, during which she can be made to carry out quite involved actions, such as making coffee, pouring drinks, and operating a record player. She has complete amnesia afterwards, unless instructed during the hypnosis that she will remember certain specified occurrences. She volunteered to take part in some ESP tests, the object of which was to determine whether scores at card-guessing made while hypnotized differed significantly from those made in her normal waking state of consciousness. Results were, on the whole, negative.

By way of relief from the tedium of card-guessing it was suggested to Miss B during hypnosis that she was a medium, and that we were about to hold a seance. (Miss B is a spiritualist, and has attended many seances.) We all duly sat with hands linked in the traditional manner (three experimenters and the subject), and Miss B went, as it were, into a trance within a trance. She gave several "messages" from purporting "communicators," some of a general nature which might well have applied to anyone, and some more specific, including names and dates, which so far have not been verified.

As the subject appeared to react more positively to this test than to card-guessing, a variation was tried at the next sitting, held a week later. Before hypnotizing Miss B I repeated to her the story of Janet's subject and the fire at Richet's laboratory. I then hypnotized her, and told her that she was able to go on "psychic excursions" just as Janet's subject had done, and that she was to go "out in her mind," find where Mr. C, one of the experimenters, lived, and describe his house to us. We were quite certain that Miss B had no idea of where Mr. C lived or what his house looked like.

After saying that she was crossing the river, Miss B declared that she was in front of the house, and described some "curves or arches" over the windows. On being told to "go in" she "went" to the rear of the house, saying that she could only enter that way. She then gave a general description of the interior, part of which could have applied to almost any house, and part definitely wrong. She did, however, comment on a large picture depicting men on horseback "fighting with spears—no, not spears—" I suggested lances, and she replied, "Yes, that's the word," and went on to describe some books on shelves, with the comment, "Over there [pointing], but I do not want to see them." She gave a distinct impression of revulsion towards the books as she said this. She could give no more information, so was told to "come back here into your body again," and awakened.

Mr. C. confirmed that his house was "over the river," and that Miss B's description of the front was remarkably good in that the house did have arched windows of a most unusual design. It was not necessary to go to the back of the house in order to enter, but entry could be made that way. Most interesting of all, however, was her description of the interior. Mr. C. did have on the wall a large painting of the battle of Waterloo, in which men on horses were depicted fighting exactly as Miss B. had described. He also had a collection of rather gruesome books on the history of capital punishment, and Miss B.'s reaction was what one might well expect from a sensitive woman at the sight of these. I should think that the odds against the subject hitting on such a combination of unusual things by sheer guesswork are, to put it mildly, rather long.

The fact that Mr. C was present and taking part in this test suggested that some telepathic process might have been involved. A further experiment, designed to eliminate this possibility, was therefore devised.

I took Miss B, by arrangement, to the house of a friend, Miss F, where another experimenter, Mr. N, was also waiting. Miss B had never met Miss F or Mr. N before, and had not visited the house previously. On our arrival she was taken into a room by Miss F, while I went with Mr. N into the room where the experiment was to take place and checked that the arrangements he had already made were complete.

Shortly before the arrival of Miss B and myself, Mr. N had walked *backwards* to a bookshelf in the experiment room and, groping with his hands behind him, had removed a book at random. This he carried behind him into an unlit adjoining room and placed under a cushion in an armchair; he then left the room and closed the door, which he kept under observation. No one entered this room again before the experiment took place. During this operation Mr. N did not see the book at all.

The subject was then brought into the experiment room by Miss F (no other persons were in the house), and the test commenced. I hypnotized Miss B and after ensuring that she was in a deep trance told her in detail what Mr. N had done. I then instructed her to go "in her mind" into the room where the book was hidden, and to tell us all she could about it.

After a few minutes of silence Miss B said that she could see the book. It was a large one, but "thin for its size." It was brown in color, and there were "some red bands—lines." In the front were the letters L and G, which, she declared, stood for the names "Leveson Gower." She could give no further information, and I terminated the hypnosis.

Mr. N fetched the book. It was, as the subject had asserted, a large thin volume, and the binding was indeed brown, although the color could not be determined without first removing a grey dust-jacket. In the front of the book, on the fly-leaf, was a handwritten inscription, in which the capital letters L and G were prominent. There was nothing, however, resembling the name Leveson Gower. There were no red bands or lines on either the book or the dust-jacket, and I was about to return the book to the shelf when, flicking through the pages, I noticed that in various places passages had been neatly underlined in red ink.

Unfortunately, circumstances prevented any repetition of these tests, and their evidential value is consequently not high. Two points are, nevertheless, worthy of note. The first is that the subject did not always seem to "see" the things she described, but in some way became directly aware of them, as with the red markings in the closed book. The second is that she not only added seemingly fictitious names to correctly perceived initials, but gave them the phonetic pronunciation "Leveson Gower." An educated Englishwoman, Miss B would most certainly, in normal circumstances, pronounce these names as "Leweson Gaw," in the approved "county" manner.

Great interest has been shown in recent reports of the work of Dr. Milan Rýzl, of Czechoslovakia, who has claimed an astonishing degree of success in developing psychic faculties in a number of subjects by the use of hypnosis. I make the following "digest" partly from published reports,[4] and partly from information which Dr. Rýzl has kindly supplied to me direct, including a paper he delivered to the Universities of Leningrad and Moscow.

In most forms of ESP research, the greatest difficulty has always been the acute and constant shortage of suitable percipients or "sensitives." From his study of the early literature of psychical research Dr. Rýzl came to the opinion that a proper application of hypnosis might go far towards a solution of this problem, and he accordingly set about devising a method of developing the psi faculty in hypnotic subjects.

Dr. Rýzl's experiments involved a total of 226 subjects, of whom seventy-three were male and 153 female, and whose ages varied between sixteen and thirty-five years. None of them, so far as he could ascertain, had ever shown the slightest sign of any psychic faculty previously, and no special methods of selection for the experiments were employed. Of this total some degree of clairvoyant ability was produced in fifty-six persons (twenty-five per cent) and of these three men and twenty-four women achieved "relatively good clairvoyant ability." Thirteen of the women achieved outstanding results, comparable to those of Dr. Rýzl's "star" subject, "Miss J. K.," to whom I shall refer later.

Although some subjects have shown a degree of clairvoyance at the first hypnosis, Dr. Rýzl makes it clear that his method is in no sense a quick and easy one. In general it involves repeated hypnoses over a considerable period. The first step, of course, is the deepening of the trance and the enhancement of suggestibility, after which comes "the exploitation of this enhanced suggestibility to obtain the necessary inhibition of cerebral activity and convincing him that he is able to acquire the ability of extra-sensory perception and that he *will* acquire it."

The subject is then given progressively complex hallucinations, first of articles well-known to him and later of less familiar and even non-existent objects, persons and scenes. This technique is continued until the "pictures" seen by the subject are as clear and distinct as a normal visual percept, and can be sustained for as long a period as the hypnotist desires. Only when this stage has been reached is the ESP training proper begun.

It is here sometimes only necessary to command the subject to ascertain something clairvoyantly in order to produce simple results. No controls are introduced at this stage, the subject merely being instructed to close his eyes and then distinguish simple objects which are placed on a tray before him. A suggestion from the hypnotist that the "picture" of the object is gradually becoming clearer is often helpful. Another method is for the hypnotist to suggest a "dream" of some scene of which it is hoped that the subject will perceive details clairvoyantly.

Once rudimentary ESP has been demonstrated advanced train ing can follow three main directions. These are, to quote Dr. Rýzl:

"(1) Development of the new abilities by giving the subject increasingly more complicated and difficult tasks. First we transfer the target to somewhere else in space. Perhaps behind the subject's back; into another room, and so on. If this proves successful we pass on to clairvoyance into different times; first into the past and then also into the future. We introduce stricter experimental conditions. We try to find out if the subject can receive aural as well as visual impressions. Also the thoughts of other people (telepathy). We also try to develop other forms of ESP, e.g., tactile forms—groping at a distance. We accustom the subject to change the place of observation as required.

"(2) We seek to remove the sources of errors in clairvoyant cognition. At first the newly developed clairvoyant ability is very imperfect, subject to a number of errors. Our subject has now to learn to resist them. Some errors have their origin in the suggestions made by the hypnotist. These are very frequent as the subject is very suggestible. It is necessary to give the subject a good deal of self-confidence by teaching him to control critically both his perceptions and the experimenter's words. Another source of errors is the influence of auto-suggestion and suppositions of the subject himself. He is influenced by previous experiences, wishes, apprehensions, presumptions as well as by the thoughts arising casually in his mind.

"In principle, the most important thing is to teach the subject how to distinguish reliably veridical hallucinations from false ones. The subject must at last learn to do this by his own reasoning. Sometimes veridical visions are distinguished by greater clarity and distinctiveness. But most often the subject must himself, by his own experience, find subjective criteria which will help him to recognize veridical visions. This is achieved by making with the subject many preliminary clairvoyant experiments in which his utterances are at once confronted with the reality, and the subject is in every case immediately informed whether he is right or wrong."

"(3) Training the subject to use his clairvoyant abilities independently of his teacher. While in the first phases of training we endeavor to enhance his suggestibility to the hypnotist's words, we now try rather to reduce it and teach him to bring himself into the hypnotic state and to control himself in it and avoid errors in making his interpretation of his clairvoyant impressions.

"This method seems to be the best for the development of ESP. It is better than the alternative of experimenting in the deepest possible hypnotic state of somnambulism where the subject, it is true, is more submitted to the experimenter's will, but where his own activity is reduced, this activity being very important in removing errors. But it implies a certain danger, for the true character of the hypnotic state is being as it were wiped off. If we prematurely give the subject too great a freedom, the hypnotic sleep becomes very superficial and the ability of ESP may disappear and the subject awakes. There is even danger we shall not succeed in hypnotizing the subject at the next attempt. For this reason a carefully successive process is necessary here until finally we may be able to educate the subject to such a perfect independence that he himself controls the depth of his sleep. Individual training of the subject is absolutely necessary so that he becomes accustomed to using his clairvoyant ability as an additional sense analogous to his other senses and in co-operation with them."

Dr. Rýzl has found that some subjects can be trained to recognize the difference between veridical and non-veridical impressions, his method here being that of suggesting to the subject that non-veridical hallucinations will be "generally indistinct, less constant and more glittering."

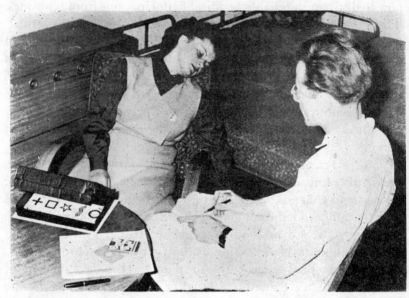

Dr. Milan Rýzl experimenting with a hypnotized subject. (Courtesy Dr. Rýzl.)

Some of his subjects have lost their ESP ability, sometimes irretrievably, after varying lengths of time. Dr. Rýzl attributes this to various incidental influences and factors mostly of a psychological nature, and does not consider that such losses are inherent in the ability itself as developed by his methods.

Miss J. K., the subject with whom Dr. Rýzl has achieved the most impressive success, is an intelligent young woman in her twenties. He describes her as honorable, reliable and energetic, but at the same time gentle and sensitive, with a strong will. She does not smoke, nor is she addicted to any "bad habits." She does not appear to have had any previous paranormal experiences. She was first hypnotized in 1958, and proved, after initial difficulty, an extremely good subject.

Under the training methods outlined above, Miss J. K. soon showed evidence of an outstanding clairvoyant faculty. Within a month she was able successfully to describe distant scenes, find lost objects, foretell the actions of strangers, and read the thoughts of other persons. Dr. Rýzl then carried out a large number of quantitative experiments in card-guessing with equally impressive results.

After considerable difficulty, Miss J. K. eventually learned to practise self-hypnosis, and about nine months after the beginning of her training reached a stage at which she could apply her ESP ability more or less at will, and quite independently of Dr. Rýzl. Here is his account of one practical example of her faculty:

"In June, 1959, in her office work several important documents of hers had been mislaid and lost. Independently of any help from me she used her clairvoyant powers and found the documents hidden away in a place hitherto unknown to her. They were in a writing desk in an office which she had last visited several months ago, and of which the appearance and arrangement had been substantially changed by extensive rebuilding. This office was several kilometres distant from the place of transfer."

Dr. Rýzl lists the following as the chief sources of error in ESP developed by his methods:

"(1) Suggestion of experimenter. This is a very serious source of errors, for the subject's suggestibility is greatly enhanced in the hypnotic state.

"(2) Auto-suggestion of the subject, the influence of his assumptions, fears, or occasional thoughts.

"(3) Illusions and hallucinations analogous to illusions in normal sensory perception.

"(4) The percepts caught are indistinct.

"(5) Influence of inattention of subject, of his being weary or his being temporarily indisposed.

"(6) Mistakes in interpretation, when the subject correctly sees the extra-sensory reality perceived, but badly interprets the meaning of the percept.

"(7) Mistakes in reproduction, when the subject clumsily reports on his percepts, so that the experimenter badly comprehends their meaning.

"(8) Telepathic influencing of the subject's percepts by persons present at the experimental sitting.

"(9) Coalescence of percepts, when two or more correct percepts referring to events somehow alike to each other, and being near to each other in time or space, coalesce into a single percept consisting of correct partial percepts, but as a whole it is wrong."

In addition to the difficulties already mentioned, Dr. Rýzl has encountered setbacks from what he terms sociological factors. First, of course, is the apprehension of many people at the idea of undergoing hypnosis, but a bigger obstacle presents itself later on, when the ESP faculty begins to develop. Contrary to what might be expected, many subjects, far from taking pleasure in gaining new abilities which, so to speak, place them above ordinary people, seem to go in fear of something which distinguishes them from others. All Dr. Rýzl's subjects were decidedly opposed to any publicity which would have made them known for their powers of extrasensory perception. Some were also apprehenhive lest this ability might bring them personal troubles and, in the case of precognition, were fearful of receiving unpleasant tidings concerning themselves.

Notwithstanding these difficulties, Dr. Rýzl considers that by his methods, "if improved and perfected, it might be possible to train the ESP ability, in greater or less degree, perhaps in all people."

In 1962, Dr. J. G. Pratt of the parapsychology laboratory of Duke University visited Dr. Rýzl, and after witnessing several series of tests agreed that "statistically significant results were obtained." The subject in these tests was a Mr. Pavel Stepánek, in whom Dr. Rýzl had recently developed the ESP faculty. The results are considered to indicate "an unusual ability of the subject to demonstrate ESP on demand under conditions that would normally be expected to inhibit successful performance."[5]

Fantastic as his results may seem, I do not think that anyone who has read his detailed reports and corresponded with Dr. Rýzl on this subject, as I have, will entertain doubts as to his sincerity and integrity. It is clearly of the greatest importance that attempts be made to duplicate his experiments in the hope of repeating his results, and in collaboration with several well-known British psychical researchers I am at present organizing such an attempt. I understand that similar experiments are also to be conducted in the U.S.A.

Interest in the application of hypnotic techniques to ESP experiments certainly seem to be increasing, and a recent paper by

C. J. Ducasse, "Hypnotism, Suggestion and Suggestibility,"[6] is a particularly valuable contribution to this branch of research. Professor Ducasse holds that hypnotism is only a special case of a familiar kind of psychological transaction, and that the state of hypnosis itself is only a temporary and exceptionally high degree of an otherwise common and quite normal psychological disposition. The process of inducing hypnosis is the *suggestion* of *suggestibility* and the production thereby of a state of *hypersuggestibility*. Suggestion, as distinct from *persuasion,* is "presentation of an idea to a mind in some manner that by-passes that mind's critical apparatus."

Discussing the nature of the hypnotic trance, Professor Ducasse makes clear the difference between hypnosis and natural sleep, and considers its relationship to spontaneous somnambulism. He also stresses the fallaciousness of the widely held belief that it is impossible, by hypnotism, to make a person perform an immoral or illegal act which he would not normally carry out. After agreeing that a hypnotized person will not *commonly* accept suggestions that are *patently* in conflict with deep moral or religious convictions, he adds:

"W. R. Wells, however, rightly holds and has experimentally demonstrated that, although Erikson and also Schilder and Kauders have contended that a hypnotized subject cannot be made to commit crimes, nevertheless such a subject *can* be made to do so if the true nature of the acts he is instructed to perform is disguised or misrepresented to him. And L. W. Rowland has proved, also experimentally, that hypnotized persons can be made to try to harm themselves or others. An excellent review and summary of the whole controversy is given by Paul C. Young who, in the light of the arguments and evidence offered by both sides, concludes that 'there is a strong presumption that a skillful hypnotist could induce antisocial behavior in hypnosis.' "

Professor Ducasse then proceeds to the consideration of hypnotism and paranormal capacities, and briefly outlines the procedure he would adopt with a hypnotized subject.

"For example, if clairvoyance should be what one is attempting to produce in the subject, he might be told that human beings have an organ for it; that ordinarily it is dormant; that it can be aroused;

and—in order to utilize the great suggestive power of ritual—that the organ will be stimulated to function when a certain spot on his head—say, between his eyebrows—has repeatedly been pressed by the hypnotist for a certain length of time. After having said this and done it, the hypnotist should then give the subject a relatively simple task of clairvoyance—for example, to look at a single playing card which is face down on the table and say of what suit it is; and, if he states it correctly, then what card of the suit it is. If the subject succeeds, then more difficult feats of clairvoyance, with strict precautions against the possibility of sensory clues, can be tried.

"If, on the other hand, the subject does not succeed, even after the purportedly clairvoyance-stimulating procedure has been repeated, then he should be given a post-hypnotic suggestion that the stimulation which has now been given the organ will persist and grow of its own momentum; and that the next time the test is given him, he will be able to read the card."

Procedures of this kind for developing in a deeply entranced subject either clairvoyance, object-reading, telepathy, or other forms of ESP are, Professor Ducasse believes, the most likely to meet with some success.

The experiments such as those of Dr. Rýzl and suggestions and ideas like those of Professor Ducasse are clearly opening an inviting and most promising avenue of inquiry, and one concerning which, I predict, much more will be heard in the not so distant future.

REFERENCES

1. Myers, F. W. H.: *Human Personality and its Survival of Bodily Death.* London, 1903.
2. Prince, Walter Franklin: Past events seership, *Proc. ASPR, 16*: Part 6.
3. Fahler, Jarl: Does hypnosis increase psychic powers?, *Tomorrow,* Autumn, 1958.
4. Rýzl, Milan: Training the psi faculty by hypnosis, *Journ. SPR, 41*: Part 711. See also *Indian Journal of Parapsychology, 2*: No. 3.
5. Rýzl, Milan, and Pratt, J. G.: Confirmation of ESP performance in a hypnotically prepared subject, *Journal of Parapsychology, 26*: No. 4.
6. Ducasse, C. J.: Hypnotism, suggestion and suggestibility, *International Journal of Parapsychology, 5*: No. 1.

Chapter 7

PARANORMAL HEALING

> *"There are natural physicians and there are artificially made physicians. The former see things which the latter cannot see, but the others dispute the existence of such things because they cannot see them. They see the exterior of things, but the true physician sees the interior. The inner man is the substantial reality; the other one is only an apparition, and therefore the true physician sees the real man and the quack only sees the illusion."*
>
> PARACELSUS

Reports of seemingly miraculous healing of the sick are as old as history. Such alleged cures take many forms, are ascribed to a great variety of causes, and range from the voodoo of witch-doctors to the miracles attributed to Christ. The Roman Catholic and other branches of the Christian Church, the Christian Scientists, the spiritualists, and many other bodies all aver that these cases of paranormal healing do occur, and in much the same way, although the explanations advanced to account for them differ widely. So divergent, indeed, are these explanations, that, granting the occurrence of the phenomena, if any one of them is right it seems the others must almost certainly be wrong—although it may well be, of course, that all are wrong and the true explanation of the phenomena is yet to be found.

I have personal cause to believe in the possibility of paranormal healing since by the use of hypnosis I have brought about a number of cures which certainly seem to defy all medical explanation. It is important to stress, however, that admitting the possibility of paranormal cures does not by any means imply accepting the explanations so far advanced for their occurrence. Many people feel unable to accept any of them; and this inability, coupled with the extravagant claims made by some "healers," seems to me the reason for one of the two main errors in this connection—namely, "throwing out the baby with the bathwater," and rejecting *all* accounts of paranormal healing because some of its trappings are questionable. A parallel to be remembered here is the scorn with which many medical men rejected hypnotism for many years in spite of the irrefutable evidence of its therapeutic value. It is hardly surprising, therefore, that paranormal healing, which is so much more difficult to demonstrate, should suffer a similar rejection. Happily, however, there have been recent indications of a growing readiness in the medical profession to consider cases on their merits and to spend time investigating them. I shall return to these later in this chapter.

The other and opposite major error in considering paranormal healing is to accept uncritically all the claims made for it. The spiritualist press in general adopts an uncritical tone which does no service to the cause it champions.

Many "healers" are, of course, completely honest and sincere, and take up the work in a genuine desire to be of service to humanity. Even those making the wildest claims—of performing "psychic operations" during trance or sleep, for example—often believe implicitly in the truth of their illusions.

Here it may be pertinent to consider three qualities a healer may possess:

1. Sincere belief in his ability to heal.
2. Actual capacity to do so.
3. Correct understanding of the methods by which such healing is effected.

A so-styled "healer" may lack all these qualities; may possess any one of the three without the others; may possess any two of them (which in practice are usually the first and second); or may conceivably possess all three. *None of these qualities implies the existence of the others.* Capacity cannot be deduced from sincerity, nor does either quality indicate understanding of the processes involved. Some "healers" show a "touchiness" towards investigators which doubtless springs from a feeling that their sincerity is being impugned. There is a regrettable amount of woolly thinking on this subject, which in my view is encouraged by the general failure in the spiritualist press to consider healers rigorously under each of these headings separately. Those who are genuinely gifted could only gain from such an approach, and charlatans would perhaps be encouraged to turn to other fields in their attempts to make an easy living.

The many advertisements by healers, appearing in issue after issue of the spiritualist press, illustrate how many rogues have jumped on the healing "band-wagon," battening on the credulity of the masses and the eternal hope of the sick for some way to relieve their sufferings. As things are, all anyone needs do—be he a rogue, a fool, or an honest person convinced that he possesses the gift of healing and genuinely anxious to help others—in order to become a "healer," is to find accommodation suitable for a "sanctuary," insert a few advertisements in the psychic newspapers, and wait for the patients, or victims, as the case may be, to roll up. If suitable premises cannot be found, or if the personality or appearance of the aspiring "healer" is unlikely to impress, he need not despair, for he can then specialize in "absent healing," in which case all he need do is "send out his healing thoughts" to those who apply for treatment. Methods of payment vary. Some "healers" ask outright for a cash payment, others insist that treatment is free, but invite free-will donations, or "love-offerings," as the Americans put it.

None of these facts can belittle the efforts of the many sincere people who believe that they have the power to heal, some of the most celebrated of whom are known personally to me, but granting that they may effect paranormal cures, even their reputations cannot but suffer from the state of affairs I have just outlined. It must be remembered also that there is a real risk of a sick person suffering grave harm through going to a "healer" instead of seeking proper medical aid, and many examples of this are on record. The following case, of which I have personal knowledge, is regrettably typical:

A woman living in America suffered from acute abdominal and back pains; she was given "spiritual healing" for these and the pain ceased to trouble her. She then came to England and joined a "group" with the object of becoming a healer herself. Within a month she had to be rushed to hospital for an emergency gall bladder operation from which she was fortunate to recover. Had she sought proper medical aid at the beginning, the crisis would probably have been averted, yet, believe it or not, the only comment from a leading member of the "healing group" was, "It may have been a lot worse if she hadn't had 'healing,' and what does it matter how it's done, so long as we got her better between us!"

Let me repeat and stress: I do not, by any means, wish to imply that there can be nothing in "spiritual" or other forms of "psychic" healing, but the fact remains that indiscriminate attempts at its practice, under whatever name, have great potential for very real harm as well as possible good.

One of the difficulties in assessing the claims of "healers" is the frequent absence of any independent diagnosis before a cure is attempted.

The "healer," who is also a medium, is often said to be helped or controlled by "spirit doctors" on "the other side." Since the diagnosis as well as the alleged cures are more often than not effected by the same "spirit doctor" or "guide," many of the more far-fetched claims made for "spiritual healing" thus remain completely unsubstantiated.

This difficulty was demonstrated by Dr. Louis Rose in his able examination of the claims made by the well-known British "healer," Harry Edwards.[1] Analysis of ninety-five claimed cures brought Dr. Rose to the following conclusions:

> In fifty-eight cases no medical or other records were available, so that the claims could not be confirmed.
>
> In twenty-two cases the claims were so much at variance with the records that further investigation was hopeless.
>
> In two cases the healer *may* have contributed to the amelioration of an organic condition.
>
> In one case organic disease was relieved after, but not necessarily as the result of, intervention by the healer.
>
> In four cases there was improvement at first but relapses followed.
>
> Four cases showed improvement in function but no improvement in the organic state.
>
> Four cases showed improvement when "healing" was being given, but orthodox medical treatment was being given at the same time.
>
> In one case the 'patient's condition, which was deter-

iorating before "healing" was given, continued to deteriorate afterwards.

In the course of his paper Dr. Rose comments on a press report that Mr. Edwards had "received his millionth letter during four-and-a-half years of healing work at Shere," observing: "Analysis of this statement reveals that Mr. Edwards and his staff must read two letters a minute over a reasonable working week, not counting time necessary for dealing with replies and instruction—*and healing.*"

It has been claimed that hypnosis can sometimes be employed not only in the treatment of disease, but in its diagnosis. Certain hypnotized subjects are said to exercise a clairvoyant faculty which enables them to name the disease from which an indicated person is suffering. The first to make such a claim seems to have been a pupil of Mesmer, the Marquis de Puysegur, who reported that a stupid peasant youth when in a deep trance showed marked clairvoyant powers, by which he was able to diagnosis the ailments of sick persons. Professor Charles Richet and Dr. Herbert Mayo, F. R. S., both eminent physiologists, are among those who have made similar claims. The latter once sent a lock of hair from one of his patients to a friend in Paris. This friend handed it to a hypnotized subject, who stated that the person from whom it came suffered from a partial paralysis of the hips and legs, and that he habitually used a surgical instrument in connection with another ailment. These statements were confirmed by Dr. Mayo as perfectly correct.

The most celebrated "psychic diagnostician" of all, however, was undoubtedly the famous Edgar Cayce (1876-1944), popularly known as the "sleeping doctor." A native of Kentucky, Cayce (pronounced Casey) lost his voice when a young man through severe laryngitis, various forms of medical treatment and several months rest failing completely to restore it.

A travelling hypnotist who treated Cayce enabled him to speak while actually under hypnosis, but attempts to render the improvement permanent by the use of post-hypnotic suggestion proved fruitless. Later, when the travelling hypnotist had left the area, a local amateur hypnotist named Layne tried the experiment of putting Cayce into a hypnotic trance, and while he was thus temporarily enabled to speak asking him why he had lost his voice and how it might be permanently restored. In answer to this question Layne was amazed to hear Cayce reply:

"Yes, we can see the body. In the normal physical state his body is unable to speak due to a partial paralysis of the vocal cord, produced by nerve strain. This is a psychological condition producing a physical effect. This may be removed by increasing the circulation to the affected part by *suggestion* while in his unconscious condition."

Layne thereupon made the necessary suggestions, and noted that Cayce's throat underwent a noticeable change of color. After a few minutes, Cayce said:

"It's all right now. The condition is removed. Make the suggestion that the circulation return to normal and after that, the body awaken."

Layne did so, and when Cayce emerged from his hypnotic state he was able to speak as well as ever. Both were so struck by this success that they decided to see if Cayce could diagnose in this way for others as well as for himself. Layne suffered from stomach trouble, and found that under hypnosis Cayce was able to diagnose it and prescribe treatment which quickly proved efficacious.

So impressed was Layne, by these results, that he became anxious to try to help others in a similar way, but Cayce, who had no medical training, was afraid that his advice might do more harm than good. At last, however, he agreed to try a few experiments with people who genuinely needed help; and when these too, proved successful, he decided to devote his life to giving what he called his "health readings."

It was found that he could make a diagnosis on a patient many miles away. He needed no details of symptoms; merely the name and address of the sufferer and the promise to be at that address at a given time. He would lie down at this time and go slowly into a trance, while Layne repeated the formula that was invariably used:

"You will now have before you (person's name), who is now at (address). You will go over this body carefully, examine it thoroughly, and tell me the conditions you find at the present time, giving the cause of existing conditions; also suggestions for the help and relief of this body. You will answer the questions as I ask them."

Should it happen that the patient was not at home as arranged, Cayce would say, "We do not have the body—we do not find him." Normally, however, he would begin, "we have the body," and would follow with a description of the patient, and often also of the patient's home and its surroundings, and of the activities of other persons in the house. He would then make a diagnosis and prescribe treatment, using accurate and highly technical medical terminology.

In his lifetime he gave more than 30,000 "readings," and came to be known as "the sleeping doctor." Not all these "readings" were correct, but most of them were amazingly accurate. When his work became widely known, many doctors applied to him in the diagnosis of difficult cases, and one of them stated that Cayce had achieved better than ninety per cent accuracy in his "readings" on the cases thus submitted.

A notable example of a successful "reading" was that made on a girl certified as insane. Cayce diagnosed that the trouble was caused by an impacted wisdom tooth impinging on a nerve in the brain, and that extraction would effect a cure. Dental examination and the extraction of the tooth concerned proved him correct, and the girl was completely restored to sanity.

Another patient was Aime Dietrich, a five-year-old in Cayce's hometown, Hopkinsville, Kentucky. After an attack of influenza when she was two, her mind had failed to develop, and she was frequently seized with convulsions. The best medical advice agreed that she was suffering from a rare brain disorder which could only prove fatal. Cayce's "reading," however, was that Aime had been injured by a fall from a carriage, and that her condition resulted from the damage caused to the injured part by her subsequent influenza attack. The osteopathic treatment he recommended proved entirely successful after a few months, and Aime's father later swore this statement:

"Our attention was called to Mr. Edgar Cayce, who was asked to diagnose her case. By autosuggestion he went into a sleep and diagnosed her case as one of congestion at the base of the brain, stating also minor details. He outlined to Dr. A. C. Layne how to proceed to cure her. Dr. Layne treated her accordingly every day for three weeks, using Mr. Cayce occasionally to follow up the treatment as results developed. Her mind began to clear up about the eighth day and within three months she was in perfect health, and is so to this day. The case can be verified by many of the best citizens of Hopkinsville, Kentucky."

The statement was endorsed: "Subscribed and sworn before me this eighth day October, 1910. Signed, D. H. Dietrich. Gerrig Raidt, Notary Public, Hamilton County, Ohio."

This case received wide publicity and thorough investigation, but without any further light being shed on Cayce's strange gift.

Later in his life, Cayce was asked to experiment in using his powers to answer questions of a religious and philosophic nature. With some hesitation he agreed, and when a questioner asked if certain events in his life could be determined by astrology, Cayce told him that they were connected with a previous life, in which he had been a monk, and not with astrology at all. Cayce, who apparently never knew afterwards what he had said during his trances, was much distressed on awakening to be told of his answer, feeling that it conflicted with his strong Christian beliefs. He was persuaded otherwise, however, and in the end gave more than two thousand "life readings," as he termed them.

Before his death in 1944, the Association for Research and Enlightenment was formed to investigate his and similar cases. Records are filed at the Association's headquarters in Virginia of all his "life readings" and of numerous reports made on them. It is claimed that research proved many of his statements to be correct.

On one occasion, Cayce stated that a certain man had previously been a Confederate soldier in the American Civil War, giving his former name and the address at which he allegedly lived. It is said that records verify the existence of a man of that name at the given address at the relevant time, who did in fact serve in the Confederate Army. If true, this certainly seems to indicate remarkable clairvoyant ability, though I shall discuss in a later chapter why it does not necessarily offer evidence of reincarnation.

The medical evidence certainly seems to indicate that Cayce had a gift for diagnosis implying an unusually accurate clairvoyance. This point has been little investigated in recent years, being passed over in favor of the more dramatic claims to direct paranormal healing. When a claim to diagnose clairvoyantly is put forward in future, whether in conjunction with a claim to heal or (more rarely) by itself, I hope it will be possible to subject it to early independent medical confirmation. The report of "non proven," necessary for example with fifty-eight out of the ninety-five cases of Harry Edward's examined by Dr. Louis Rose, and so unsatisfactory to the healer and the investigator alike, might then be avoided in a higher proportion of cases.

A thorough enquiry into the "miracles" of Lourdes, made by Dr. D. J. West, a former research officer of the SPR, produced similarly disappointing results.[2] Dr. West confined his investigation to eleven cases which the Church had officially pronounced miraculous cures of organic diseases. His report makes it abundantly clear that there is no real evidence to warrant the term "miracle" in connection with any of them.

It has often been noted that the degree of suggestibility of the subject exerts a definite influence on the outcome, and this principle seems undoubtedly to lie behind the cures effected by Christian Scientists and "spiritual" healers, and the "miracles" of religious shrines such as Lourdes. The conditions associated with these—tense religious atmosphere, expectancy, etc.—are all such as would increase the suggestibility of the patient to a high degree, and the illnesses that seem to be cured in these circumstances are almost invariably of the type known to be curable by hypnotic suggestion.

Many claims have been made that cures of an apparently paranormal kind have been effected by the use of hypnotism, most of them, unfortunately, lacking reliable authentication. Particular interest was aroused, therefore, both in medical and parapsychological circles, when a report of such a cure, signed by no less an authority than Dr. A. A. Mason, Senior Registrar at the Queen Victoria Hospital, East Grinstead, was published in 1952.[3]

The patient, a youth of sixteen, suffered from congenital ichthyosis, commonly known as "crocodile skin," an inherited condition normally regarded as incurable. A black, horny layer covered his entire body except his chest, neck and face. In Dr. Mason's words:

"The skin was papilliferous, each papilla projecting 2-6 mm. above the surface, and the papillae were separated from each other by only a very small distance, perhaps 1 mm. The papillae themselves varied in size from small thread-like projections on the abdomen, back and flexor surfaces of the arms to large warty excrescences 5 mm. across on the feet, thighs and palms. The small amount of skin which was visible between the papillae was also black, horny, and fissured. To the touch the skin felt as hard as a normal finger-nail, and was so inelastic that any attempt at bending resulted in a crack in the surface, which would then ooze blood-stained serum. In the skin flexures there were fissures which were constantly being reopened by movement and were chronically infected and painful. The ichthyosiform layer, when cut, was of the consistence of cartilage and was anaesthetic for a depth of several millimetres.

"The condition varied in severity in different areas of the body, being worst on the hands, feet, thighs, and calves, and least on the upper arms, abdomen, and back. The skin on the face, neck, and chest appeared normal, although, as is shown later, it became papilliferous when transplanted to the palms."

The patient had been treated at various hospitals without avail, and skin grafting had proved ineffective. Dr. Mason therefore decided to try the effect of hypnosis, confining his suggestions in the first instance to the left arm in order to exclude the possibility of spontaneous resolution. "About five days later," states Dr. Mason, "the horny layer softened, became friable, and fell off. The skin underneath was slightly erythematous, but normal in texture and color. From a black and armour-like casing, the skin became pink and soft within a few days. Improvement occurred first in the flexures and areas of friction, and later on the rest of the arm. The erythema faded in a few days. At the end of 10 days the arm was completely clear from shoulder to wrist."

Dr. Mason then extended the treatment to the rest of the youth's body with almost equal success, as the following table shows:

Region	Before Treatment	After Treatment
Hands	Completely covered	Palms clear. Fingers not greatly improved
Arms	80% covered	95% cleared
Back	Covered, but only lightly	90% cleared
Buttocks	Heavily covered	60% cleared
Thighs	Completely and heavily covered	70% cleared
Legs and Feet	Completely and heavily covered	50% cleared

During the first few weeks of hypnotic treatment the improvement was "rapid and dramatic," after which there was no appreciable change during several months. After a year, however, there was no relapse whatever of the improved areas.

The power of suggestion has achieved widespread medical recognition in recent years, to such an extent that it may soon not be regarded as "paranormal" at all. This ironical development is adumbrated in a report (published in 1956, a few years after Dr. Mason's paper) by a committee appointed by the British Medical Association to investigate the claims of spiritual healers. Its report included the following statement:

"As far then as our investigation and observation have gone, we have no evidence that there is any special type of illness cured solely by spiritual healing which cannot be cured by medical methods which do not involve such claims. The cases claimed as cures of a miraculous nature present no features of a unique and unexpected character outside the knowledge of any experienced physician or psychiatrist. . . . We find that, whilst patients suffering from psychogenic disorders may be 'cured' by various methods of spiritual healing, just as they are by methods of suggestion and other forms of psychological treatment employed by doctors, we can find no evidence that organic diseases are cured solely by such means. The evidence suggests that many cases claimed to be cured are likely to be either instances of wrong diagnosis, wrong prognosis, remission or possibility of spontaneous cure."

Following Dr. Mason's report on his "crocodile skin" cure, hypnosis has since been employed with no less spectacular success in the alleviation of similar conditions by others, notably by C. A. S. Wink, of Oxford, who reported the successful treatment of two cases of congenital ichthyosiform erythrodermia in 1961.[4] Dr. Wink's patients were sisters, aged eight and six respectively, who had previously been treated without success by more orthodox methods. His report is particularly valuable in that it throws some light on the *modus operandi* of hypnotic treatment in such cases.

The most recent experiments in the field of paranormal healing were devised as a joint project by the Allen Memorial Institute, McGill University, Montreal, and the Department of Physiology of the University of Manitoba.

These tests show a departure from the use of suggestion, usually under hypnosis, which has featured in most of the recent work on the subject. They appear to show conclusively that a certain healer was able to cause a significant speeding up of the healing process in a carefully controlled group of mice upon which skin wounds had been inflicted. A report by Dr. Carroll B. Nash contains the following concise summary:

"A healer held between his hands, for two fifteen-minute periods a day, ten cages, each containing ten wounded mice in separate compartments. The cage was concealed in an open paper bag into which the healer inserted his hands without looking at mice or cage. A second group of wounded mice was treated in the same way except that a different individual held the cage each day, and a third group of wounded mice remained unhandled. Each group consisted of a hundred mice in ten different cages. The rate of healing was significantly greater in the group held by the healer than it was in the other two groups, and there was no significant difference between the rates of healing in the latter two. (The mean wound area on the sixteenth day following wounding was .013 square inch for the group held by the healer, and .026 and .022 square inch, respectively, for the second and third groups.)"[5]

From the investigator's point of view, this is better evidence for the claims of healers than has yet been provided by any direct examination of their human subjects. Since medical interest in paranormal healing now seems securely aroused, and since the center of interest in the spiritualist movement seems to have shifted largely from mediumistic communication to paranormal, or allegedly "spiritual" healing, it is to be hoped that similar work, of interest and possible benefit to all sides will be undertaken increasingly in the future.

REFERENCES

1. Rose, Louis: Some aspects of paranormal healing, *Journ. SPR, 38*: 105-121.
2. West, Donald J.: *Eleven Lourdes Miracles.* London, 1957.
3. Mason, A. A.: A case of congenital ichthyosiform erythrodermia of brocq treated by hypnosis, *British Medical Journal,* No. 4781, pp. 422-3. (See also *Journ. SPR, 36*:716-8.)
4. Wink, C. A. S.: Congenital ichthyosiform erythrodermia treated by hypnosis, *British Medical Journal,* 2:741-3.
5. Nash, Carroll B.: Medical implications of parapsychology, *International Journal of Parapsychology, 4*: 3:5-16.

Chapter 8

DOES MAN SURVIVE DEATH?

*"The question for man most momentous of all is whether
or no he has an immortal soul; or—to avoid the word
immortal, which belongs to the realm of infinities—
whether or no his personality involves any element which
can survive bodily death. In this direction have always
lain the gravest fears, the farthest reaching hopes, which
could either oppress or stimulate mortal minds."*

F. W. H. MYERS

THE QUOTATION ABOVE is from Myers's introduction to his great
work, *Human Personality and Its Survival of Bodily Death*. The
view expressed was certainly true of Myers, and it is undoubtedly
in the hope of finding an answer to this question that many people
turn to the study of psychical research. This, indeed, was the pri-
mary interest of most of the founders of the SPR, and as we have
seen, much of the early work of that society was concerned with the
investigation of ghostly appearances, hauntings, mediumistic phenomena and other occurrences commonly attributed to discarnate
spirits.

Disregarding the more credulous type of spiritualist, who
attributes to spirit intervention practically everything that appears
to be paranormal (and much that is capable of explanation in perfectly normal terms) there have been, and still are, many serious
students of the subject who consider that certain phenomena are
only to be reasonably explained on the hypothesis of survival and
communication. In this chapter I shall give examples of the sort
of evidence that convinced such eminent thinkers as Frederic
Myers, Sir Oliver Lodge, Mrs. Henry Sidgwick, Sir William Barrett,
Richard Hodgson and Professor J. H. Hyslop. Much of this evidence is in the form of reports of spontaneous experiences, and
most of the rest is provided by information received through mediums—for instance the famous "R.101" case described in a preceding chapter. The spontaneous experiences are usually in the form

of visual hallucinations or "apparitions." One of the most striking and best authenticated examples is the "scratched cheek case" cited by Myers in *Human Personality*.[1] In this case it seems that the apparition of a woman, who had died nine years previously, appeared to warn her brother of their mother's impending death. It was first reported to the American SPR, and the integrity of all the persons concerned was vouched for by Professor Josiah Royce and by Richard Hodgson. The first report, dated January 11, 1888, was as follows:

"Sir,—Replying to the recently published request of your Society for actual occurrences of psychical phenomena, I respectfully submit the following remarkable occurrence to the consideration of your distinguished Society, with the assurance that the event made a more powerful impression on my mind than the combined incidents of my whole life. I have never mentioned it outside of my family and a few intimate friends, knowing well that few would believe it, or else ascribe it to some disordered state of mind at the time; but I well know I never was in better health or possessed a clearer head and mind than at the time it occurred.

In 1867, my only sister, a young lady of eighteen years, died suddenly of cholera in St. Louis, Mo. My attachment for her was very strong, and the blow a severe one to me. A year or so after her death the writer became a commercial traveller, and it was in 1876, while on one of my Western trips, that the event occurred.

"I had 'drummed' the city of St. Joseph, Mo., and had gone to my room at the Pacific House to send in my orders, which were unusually large ones, so that I was in a very happy frame of mind indeed. My thoughts, of course, were about these orders, knowing how pleased my house would be at my success. I had not been thinking of my late sister, or in any manner reflecting on the past. The hour was high noon, and the sun was shining cheerfully into my room. While busily smoking a cigar and writing out my orders, I suddenly became conscious that some one was sitting on my left, with one arm resting on the table. Quick as a flash I turned and distinctly saw the form of my dead sister, and for a brief second or so looked her squarely in the face; and so sure was I that it was she, that I sprang forward in delight, calling her by name, and as I did so, the apparition instantly vanished. Naturally, I was startled and dumbfounded, almost doubting my senses; but with the cigar in my mouth, and pen in hand, with the ink still moist on my letter, I satisfied myself I had not been dreaming and was wide awake. I was near enough to touch her, had it been a physical possibility, and noted her features, expression, and details of dress, etc. She appeared as if alive. Her eyes looked kindly and perfectly natural into mine. Her skin was so life-like that I could see the glow or moisture on its surface, and, on the whole, there was no change in her appearance, otherwise than when alive.

"Now comes the most remarkable confirmation of my statement, which cannot be doubted by those who know what I state actually occurred. This visitation, or whatever you may call it, so impressed me that I took the next train home, and in the presence of my parents and others I related what had occurred. My father, a man of rare good sense and very practical, was inclined to ridicule me, as he saw how earnestly I believed what I stated; but he, too, was amazed when later on I told them of a bright red line or scratch on the right-hand side of my sister's face, which I distinctly had seen. When I mentioned this my mother rose trembling to her feet and nearly fainted away, and as soon as she sufficiently recovered her self-possession, with tears streaming down her face, she explained that I had indeed seen my sister, as no living mortal but herself was aware of that scratch, which she had accidentally made while doing some little act of kindness after my sister's death. She said she well remembered how pained she was to think she should have, unintentionally, marred the features of her dead daughter, and that, unknown to all, how she had carefully obliterated all traces of the slight scratch with the aid of powder, etc., and that she had never mentioned it to a human being from that day to this. In proof, neither my father nor any of our family had detected it, and positively were unaware of the incident, yet I saw the scratch as bright as if just made. So strangely impressed was my mother, that even after she had retired to rest she got up and dressed, came to me and told me she knew at least that I had seen my sister. A few weeks later my mother died, happy in her belief she would rejoin her favorite daughter in a better world."

In a further letter Mr. F. G. added:

"There was nothing of a spiritual or ghostly nature in either the form or dress of my sister, she appearing perfectly natural, and dressed in clothing that she usually wore in life, and which was familiar to me. From her position at the table, I could only see her from the waist up, and her appearance and everything she wore is indelibly photographed in my mind. I even had time to notice the collar and little breast-pin she wore, as well as the comb in her hair, after the style then worn by young ladies. The dress had no particular association for me or my mother, no more so than others she was in the habit of wearing; but today, while I have forgotten all her other dresses, pins, and combs, I could go to her trunk (which we have just as she left it) and pick out the very dress and ornaments she wore when she appeared to me, so well do I remember it.

"You are correct in understanding that I returned home earlier than I had intended, as it had such an effect on me that I could hardly think of any other matter; in fact, I abandoned a trip that I had barely commenced, and, ordinarily, would have remained on the road a month longer."

Mr. F. G. again wrote to Dr. Hodgson, 23rd January, 1888:

"As per your request, I enclose a letter from my father which is endorsed by my brother, confirming the statement I made to them of the apparition I had seen. I will add that my father is one of the oldest and most respected citizens of St. Louis, Mo., a retired merchant, whose winter residence is at _____, Ill., a few miles out by rail. He is now seventy years of age, but a remarkably well-preserved gentleman in body and mind, and a very learned man as well. As I informed you, he is slow to believe things that reason cannot explain. My brother, who endorses the statement, has resided in Boston for twelve years, doing business on _____ Street, as per letter-head above, and the last man in the world to take stock in statements without good proof. The others who were present (including my mother) are now dead, or were then so young as to now have but a dim remembrance of the matter.

"You will note that my father refers to the 'scratch,' and it was this that puzzled all, even himself, and which we have never been able to account for, further than that in some mysterious way I had actually seen my sister nine years after death, and had particularly noticed and described to my parents and family this bright red scratch, and which, beyond all doubt in our minds, was unknown to a soul save my mother, who had accidentally caused it.

"When I made my statement, all, of course, listened and were interested; but the matter would probably have passed with comments that it was a freak of memory had not I asked about the scratch, and the instant I mentioned it my mother was aroused as if she had received an electric shock, as she had kept it a secret from all, and she alone was able to explain it. My mother was a sincere Christian lady, who was for twenty-five years superintendent of a large infant class in her church, The Southern Methodist, and a directress in many charitable institutions, and was highly educated. No lady at the time stood higher in the city of St. Louis, and she was, besides, a woman of rare good sense.

"I mention these points to give you an insight into the character and standing of those whose testimony, in such a case, is necessary. (Signed) F. G."

From Mr. H. G.:

"Dear F.,—Yours of 16th inst. is received. In reply to your questions relating to your having seen our Annie, while at St. Joseph, Mo., I will state that I well remember the statement you made to family on your return home. I remember your stating how she looked in ordinary home dress, and particularly about the scratch (or red spot) on her face, which you could not account for, but which was fully explained by your mother. The spot was made while adjusting something about her head while in the casket, and covered with powder. All who heard you relate the phenomenal sight thought it was true. You well know how sceptical I am about things which reason cannot explain. (Signed) H. G. (father).

"I was present at the time and indorse the above.

(Signed) K. G. (brother)."

Here, Myers commented:

"The apparent redness of the scratch on the face of the apparition goes naturally enough with the look of life in the face. The phantom did not appear as a corpse, but as a blooming girl, and the scratch showed as it would have shown if made during life."

Dr. Hodgson visited Mr. F. G. later, and sent the following notes of his interview:

"St. Louis, Mo., April 16, 1890.

"In conversation with Mr. F. G., now forty-three years of age, he says that there was a very special sympathy between his mother, sister, and himself.

"When he saw the apparition he was seated at a small table, about two feet in diameter, and had his left elbow on the table. The scratch which he saw was on the right side of his sister's nose, about three-fourths of an inch long, and was a somewhat ragged mark. His home at the time of the incident was in St. Louis. His mother died within two weeks after the incident. His sister's face was hardly a foot away from his own. The sun was shining upon it through the open window. The figure disappeared like an instantaneous evaporation.

"Mr. G. has had another experience, but of a somewhat different character. Last fall the impression persisted for some time of a lady friend of his, and he could not rid himself for some time of thoughts of her. He found afterwards that she died at the time of the curious persistence of his impression.

"Mr. G. appears to be a first-class witness. (Signed) R. Hodgson."

Myers commented:

"I have ranked this case primâ facie as a perception by the spirit of her mother's approaching death. That coincidence is too marked to be explained away: the son is brought home in time to see his mother once more by perhaps the only means which would have succeeded; and the mother herself is sustained by the knowledge that her daughter loves and awaits her. I think that the very fact that the apparition was not that of the corpse with the full mark on which the mother's regretful thoughts might dwell, but was that of the girl in health and happiness, with the symbolic red mark worn simply as a test of identity, goes far to show that it was not the mother's mind from whence that image came. As to the spirit's own knowledge of the fate of the body after death, there are other cases which show, I think, that this specific form of post-mortem perception is not unusual.

"However explained, the case is one of the best-attested, and in itself one of the most remarkable, that we possess."

Spontaneous experiences of this kind sometimes take the form of dreams. The best known is the "Chaffin Will case" in which the visionary appearance of a dead man led to the discovery of a hitherto unknown will. This case is also one of the best authenticated, for the facts were all examined in a court of justice. On November 16, 1905, James A. Chaffin, a farmer of Davie County, North Carolina, made a will, attested by two witnesses, leaving his estate to his third son, Marshall, whom he appointed sole executor. No provision was made for his wife or his three other sons. On January 16, 1919, he made a second will directing that his property should be divided equally between his four sons. This will was unattested, but according to North Carolina law would be valid if it were proved to have been written entirely by the testator. So far as is known he never disclosed the existence of this will during his lifetime. On September 7, 1921, Chaffin was killed by a fall. Marshall, the third son, obtained probate of the first will, which was not contested. Four years later, the second son, James P. Chaffin, had several dreams in which his father appeared and spoke to him. Here is an extract from a sworn statement made to an SPR investigator J. MacNeill Johnson:

"In all my life I never heard my father mention having made a later will than the one dated in 1905. I think it was in June of 1925 that I began to have very vivid dreams that my father appeared to me at my bedside but made no verbal communication. Some time later, I think it was the latter part of June, 1925, he appeared at my bedside again, dressed as I had often seen him dressed in life, wearing a black overcoat which I knew to be his own. This time my father's spirit spoke to me, he took hold of his overcoat this way and pulled it back and said, 'You will find my will in my overcoat pocket,' and then disappeared. The next morning I arose fully convinced that my father's spirit had visited me for the purpose of explaining some mistake. I went to mother's and looked for the overcoat but found that it was gone. Mother stated that she had given the overcoat to my brother John who lives in Yadkin County about twenty miles northwest of my home.

I think it was on the 6th July, which was on Monday following the events stated in the last paragraph, I went to my brother's home in Yadkin County and found the coat. On examination of the inside pocket I found that the lining had been sewed together. I immediately cut the stitches and found a little roll of paper tied with a string which was in my father's handwriting and contained only the following words: 'Read the 27th chapter of Genesis in my daddie's old Bible.'

"At this point I was so convinced that the mystery was to be cleared up I was unwilling to go to mother's home to examine the old Bible without the presence of a witness and I induced a neighbor, Thomas Blackwelder, to accompany me, also my daughter and Mr. Blackwelder's daughter were present. Arriving at mother's home we had a considerable search before we found the old Bible. At last we did find it in the top drawer in an upstairs room. The book was so dilapidated that when we took it out it fell into three pieces. Mr. Blackwelder picked up the portion containing the Book of Genesis and turned the leaves until he came to the 27th chapter of Genesis and there we found two leaves folded together, the left hand page folded to the right and the right hand page folded to the left forming a pocket and in this pocket Mr. Blackwelder found the will which has been probated.

"During the month of December, 1925, my father again appeared to me about a week before the trial of the case of Chaffin vs. Chaffin and said 'Where is my old will,' and showed considerable temper. I believed from this that I would win the lawsuit as I did. I told my lawyer about this visitation the next morning. Many of my friends do not believe it is possible for the living to hold communication with the dead but I am convinced that my father actually appeared to me on these several occasions and I shall believe it to the day of my death."

According to MacNeill Johnson, who made an extensive on-the-spot investigation, James P. Chaffin, his wife and daughter, Thomas Blackwelder and his daughter, and James L. Chaffin's widow were all present when the Bible containing the will was found.

This second will was tendered for probate. Marshall, the benefactor under the first, had died a year after his father, and his widow and son appeared in court to contest it. When ten witnesses declared that the will was in James L. Chaffin's own handwriting, however, they withdrew their opposition and probate was granted. A detailed report of the cases in SPR *Proceedings* concluded with these comments:

"So much for the facts stated in the documents. In considering whether they can be accounted for without recourse to the supernormal, we must rule out any explanation which presupposes either that the second will was a 'fake' or that any of the parties interested under the second will had normal knowledge of its existence prior to Mr. J. P. Chaffin's and Mr. Blackwelder's search for the old Bible in July, 1925.

"As to the hypothesis of a fake, it is indeed curious that Chaffin should have been so anxious to remedy the injustice done by the first will as to make a second will on entirely different lines, and at the same time have been so remiss in taking precautions during his lifetime for the carrying into effect of his second will. Possibly he intended to reveal its existence on his death-bed, and the circumstances of his death as the result of an accident frustrated his intention. But the fact that ten witnesses were prepared to swear that the second will was in the testator's handwriting, and that Marshall's widow and son, after seeing the document, admitted its genuineness, seems decisively to negative any hypothesis of a 'fake' will. Moreover, Mr. Johnson, who interviewed and questioned Mr. J. P. Chaffin, his wife, mother and daughter in April, 1927, was, to use his own words, 'much impressed with the evident sincerity of these people, who had the appearance of honest, honorable country people, in well-to-do circumstances.'

"Mr. Johnson in his statement suggests, only to dismiss, another possible explanation. 'I endeavoured with all my skill and ability by cross-examination and otherwise to induce some admission that possibly there was a subconscious knowledge of the Will in the old Bible, or of the paper in the coat pocket, that was brought to the fore by the dream: but I utterly failed to shake their faith. The answer was a quiet: "Nay: such an explanation is impossible. We never heard of the existence of the will till the visitation from my father's spirit." Clearly, none of them had any conscious recollection, at the date of the testator's death, of any mention of a second will, or they would not have allowed the first to be proved without opposition. Nor was it a matter which, if once mentioned, they were likely to forget, during the short period which intervened between the making of the second will (January, 1919) and the testator's death (September, 1921). The hypothesis therefore of the "exterioralization' in the form of a vision, of knowledge normally acquired by Mr. J. P. Chaffin, but only remembered subconsciously, is open to grave objection.

"It is hard to suggest a satisfactory explanation of the facts on normal lines. If a supernormal explanation be accepted, it is to be noted that the present case is of a comparatively infrequent type, in which more than one of the percipient's senses is affected by the phantasm. Mr. J. P. Chaffin both 'saw' his father and 'heard' him speak. The auditory impression was not strictly accurate: what was in the overcoat pocket was not the second will, but a clue to its whereabouts; but the practical result was the same. Mr. Johnson was unable to obtain a clear statement from Mr. J. P. Chaffin as to whether he was awake or asleep at the time of the apparition. He first said he was awake but on a 'rather rigid examination' admitted that he might have been in a doze. Mr. Johnson says, 'I believe he does not know himself.' "[2]

Many parapsychologists do not accept that cases of the Chaffin type are evidence of survival, however. For instance, in an article in the SPR *Journal* for December, 1962, the well-known Dutch researcher George Zorab outlines this case and a number of similar ones, and goes on to show why, in his opinion, they do not really constitute evidence of survival, but rather of clairvoyance. He bases his argument largely on what he terms the "Dordrecht case," the basic facts of which are as follows:

A man had held a position as bookkeeper to a large firm for many years and was trusted and highly respected by his employers. One day, however, a deficit amounting to some 1,800 guilders was discovered, for which, despite a thorough check of his figures, the bookkeeper was unable to account. The suspicion, amounting almost to accusation of embezzlement, which fell upon him brought on a fatal illness, but he declared his innocence to the end, charging his sons to spare no effort in clearing his name. There seemed to be no way of doing this, however, and the deficit was paid off by his heirs.

Shortly afterwards one of the sons had a hallucinatory dream wherein a white figure, which he did not recognize, entered his room and came to his bed, saying repeatedly, "Look in the ledger at the dates." Realizing that the apparition was connected with his father, the son went next day to the employers and obtained permission to examine the relevant books. Sure enough, on one page he found that the date had been included in the addition of a column of figures, thus increasing the total figure by the exact amount thought to be missing.

Zorab argues that in this case we have a paranormal experience in which information unknown to anybody, either in the past or the present, was conveyed to the percipient. The manner in which the information was brought to the knowledge of the percipient was almost identical with other cases of the Chaffin Will type, except that in the Dordrecht case the information was passed on in the dream by a mysterious, unrecognized, white figure. He concludes:

"In short, I would like to make the point that in reality not the slightest difference exists between the mysterious white figure of the Dordrecht case and the recognized deceased entities of the other cases quoted. All these entities, appearing in the various dreams, whether recognized or unrecognized, are but constructions of the same fabulating capacity of our dream consciousness. From this point of view the Dordrecht apparition was no spirit, nor James L. Chaffin, deceased, appearing in his son's dream. The bits of information paranormally received were passed on to the various percipients, dressed up in the personifications best adapted to convince the dreamer of its veridical nature and thus urging him to act upon the information received in a manner apparently supernatural to the percipient.

"In view of what has been stated above, I would like to suggest that the Dordrecht case clearly indicates that if in a dream or vision a deceased person appears giving information only known to himself when alive, such a case in no way constitutes sound evidence for the survival of that person's personality. Such cases can be better classified as evidence for clairvoyance, if we are sure that no normal psychological factors can be brought forward as an explanation of the phenomena."[3]

I have already mentioned the conviction of Sir Oliver Lodge that he had received communications through mediums from his son Raymond, who was killed in the first World War. Here is an example of the sort of evidence that convinced Lodge.

Raymond Lodge was killed in action on September 14, 1915. A fortnight later his mother, Lady Lodge, had an anonymous sitting with a well known professional medium, A. Vout Peters, in the course of which the following was received:

"You have several portraits of this boy. Before he went away you had got a good portrait of him—two—no, three. Two where he is alone and one where he is in a group with other men. He is particular that I should tell you of this. In one you see his walking-stick." Here the medium put an imaginary stick under his arm.

The Lodges had photographs of Raymond, but in none of these was he one of a group, and Lady Lodge was sceptical, thinking it was likely to be just a guess by the medium at something probable. Two days later, however, a letter was received from a Mrs. Cheves, who was a stranger to them but whose son had been at the front with Raymond. It said:

"Dear Lady Lodge,—My son who is M.O. to the 2nd South Lancs., has sent us a group of officers taken in August, and I wondered whether you knew of this photo and had had a copy. If not may I send you one, as we have half a dozen and also a key? I hope you will forgive my writing to ask this, but I have often thought of you and felt so much for you in your great sorrow.—Sincerely yours, B. P. Cheves."

The Lodges replied immediately accepting the offer, but fortunately, as it transpired, the photograph was not received until the afternoon of December 7. On December 6, Lady Lodge was looking through Raymond's diary, which had been returned with his kit, and found an entry made on August 4, "Photo taken." Raymond had never mentioned this in his letters, and as far as is known he had never seen a print. On the morning of December 7 a letter arrived from Mrs. Cheves saying that the photograph was being dispatched. As soon as this letter was received Lodge sent a letter to a friend, J. Arthur Hill, who was also a well-known researcher, recording his impressions of what the photograph would be like. These impressions were gained from a sitting which Lodge had with the medium Mrs. Osborn Leonard on December 3. The letter ran:

"Concerning that photograph which Raymond mentioned through Peters [Hill had seen the record of this sitting], he has said some more about it through Mrs. Leonard. But he is doubtful about the stick. What he says is that there is a considerable number of men in the photograph; that the front row is sitting, and that there is a back row, or some of the people grouped and set up at the back; also that there are a dozen or more people in the photograph, and that some of them he hardly knew; that a B is prominent in the photograph, and that there is also a C; that he himself is sitting down, and that there are people behind him, one of whom either leant on his shoulder, or tried to.

"The photograph has not come yet, but it may come any day now; so I send this off before I get it.

"The actual record of what was said in the sitting is being typed, but the above represents my impression of it."

The photograph was delivered between 3 and 4 p.m. that day. Lodge found that "every peculiarity mentioned by Raymond [through the mediums] was strikingly correct." The walking-stick was there, and six prominent vertical battens on the roof of a shed in the background corresponded with a description by Mrs. Leonard's "control," who had by gesture emphasized vertical lines. Lodge's account continues:

"By a 'mixed lot,' we understood members of different Companies—not all belonging to Raymond's Company, but a collection from the several. This must be correct, as they are too numerous for one Company. As to 'prominence,' I have asked several people which member of the group seemed to them the most prominent, and except as regards central position, a well-lighted standing figure on the right has usually been pointed to as most prominent. This one is 'B' as stated.

"Some of the officers must have been barely known to Raymond, while some were his friends. Officers whose names begin with B, with C, and R were among them; there was not any name beginning with K, but there is a name beginning with a hard C.

"Some of the group are sitting while others are standing behind. Raymond is one of those sitting, and his walking-stick or regulation cane is lying across his feet. The background is dark, and is conspicuously lined. It is out of doors, close in front of a shed or military hut, pretty much as suggested to me by the statements made in the 'Leonard' sitting—what I called a 'shelter.'

"But by far the most striking piece of evidence is the fact that some one sitting behind Raymond is leaning or resting a hand on his shoulder. The photograph fortunately shows the actual occurrence, and almost indicates that Raymond was rather annoyed with it; for his face is a little screwed up, and his head has been slightly bent to one side out of the way of the man's arm. It is the only case in the photograph where one man is leaning or resting his hand on the shoulder of another, and I judge that it is a thing not unlikely to be remembered by the one to whom it occurred.

"Through information supplied by Mrs. Cheves I obtained prints of all the accessible photographs which had been taken at the same time. I found that the group had been repeated, with slight variations, three times—the officers all in the same relative positions but not in identically the same attitudes. One of them is the same as the one we had seen, with his hand resting on Raymond's shoulder, and Raymond's head leaning a little on one side, as if rather annoyed. In another the hand had been removed, being supported by a stick, and in that one Raymond's head is upright. This corresponds to his uncertainty as to whether he was actually taken with the man leaning on him or not. In a third variation, however, Captain S's leg rests on or touches Raymond's shoulder, and the slant of the head and slight look of annoyance have returned.

"As to the evidential value of the whole communication, it will be observed that there is something of the nature of cross-correspondence, of a simple kind, in the fact that a reference to the photograph was made by one medium, and details given by another in answer to a question which I had asked about it: the communicator showing awareness that previous reference was made through another channel.

"And the elimination of ordinary telepathy from the living, except under the far-fetched hypothesis of the unconscious influence of complete strangers, was exceptionally complete; inasmuch as the whole of the information was recorded before any of us had seen the photograph."[4]

Much of the best survival evidence is from "automatic writing." Sometimes this is produced with the aid of a "planchette" —a heart-shaped piece of wood with a pencil projecting through a hole at the pointed end—or a "ouija-board," but many automatists merely hold a pen or pencil in the normal manner. The writing is usually produced in a state differing from normal consciousness, which may be anything between mild dissociation and deep trance, and the automatist rarely seems aware of what he is writing. Most automatic writing is nothing more than the product of the automatist's own unconsciousness, but occasionally information is given in this manner which the writer could not seemingly have acquired by any normal means. Here is a particularly dramatic example:

During the first World War an automatist who believed that her writing was dictated by a friend killed in action was informed in this manner that another deceased person wished to communicate. The style of writing changed and she wrote: "Fear led me to do a very evil thing. I cannot forgive myself." In answer to questions, the "spirit" gave his name as Whiteman, wrote the name of his school, and added that he had died about fifty years before but had no grave. He was unhappy because he had attempted to escape death at the expense of another. He said he had been a clergyman. Asked where he had died he replied, "London." Enquiries were made, and it was found that a man named Whiteman had been at the college named. He was born in 1829, had become a clergyman, and was on his way to Australia when he was lost in the *S.S. London,* which had foundered in the Bay of Biscay in 1866, just fifty years before. Reference to the sailing list of the *S.S. London* confirmed that he was a passenger, and independent confirmation was obtained that a Reverend John Whiteman had died in 1866. The automatist was certain that she had never known of the loss of the *S.S. London.*[5]

The most famous cases of automatic writing and those most frequently cited as evidence of survival are, without doubt, the "cross-correspondences" of a team of automatists usually known as the "SPR Group," which began in 1901, and continued until after 1930. The term "group" is not a strictly accurate description, since its members never met as a body, were in most cases hardly known to each other, and in some cases never even met as individuals. The principal members were: Mrs. A. W. Verrall, a classical scholar and a close friend of F. W. H. Myers; Miss Helen Verrall, daughter of Mrs. Verrall and later Mrs. W. H. Salter; "Mrs. Holland," later revealed to be Mrs. Fleming, sister of Rudyard Kipling; "Mrs. Willett," later revealed to be Mrs. Coombe-Tennant; "Mrs. King," later revealed to be Dame Edith Lyttelton; Mrs. Stuart Wilson; and the American trance medium, Mrs. Piper, the only professional medium in the group. Their "scripts" include, in addition to automatic writing, some records of trance statements and of visual impressions received in "borderline" states of dissociation.

Shortly after the death of Myers in 1901, Mrs. Verrall, keenly interested in psychical research, began trying to develop automatic writing in order to give Myers, if he still existed, a chance to demonstrate the fact. After a few months she began to produce more or less lucid scripts purporting to come from Myers. Though they were largely in Latin and Greek they fell far below the standards of scholarship of both Myers and herself. They improved slowly, however, although their meaning remained obscure. Then, about a year later, Mrs. Piper in America also began to give messages purportedly from Myers, and it was found that these contained allusions to some of the material in Mrs. Verrall's scripts. Soon afterwards Miss Helen Verrall began to produce automatic writing, and although she had not seen her mother's scripts, she too referred to the same subjects as Mrs. Verrall and Mrs. Piper. These and all subsequent scripts were sent to the SPR where they were filed.

In 1903 "Mrs. Holland," who was then living in India, also began to produce scripts purporting to come from Myers. One of the scripts contained instructions to send it to Mrs. Verrall, and gave her address—5, Selwyn Gardens, Cambridge—correctly. Now Mrs. Holland had never met Mrs. Verrall, although she may have remembered her name, mentioned in Myers's *Human Personality,* which Mrs. Holland had read. She had never been to Cambridge, nor did she recall ever having heard of Selwyn Gardens. Instead of obeying the instructions she sent the script, together with several others, to the SPR. Although the fact was not at first realized, these documents also contained veiled allusions to the same subjects as those in the scripts of Mrs. Verrall, Miss Helen Verrall and Mrs. Piper. Other members of the "SPR Group" later added material which also seemed to fit in the same way, until the scripts eventually reached a total of more than 3,000 documents.

The study and interpretation of the scripts formed a gigantic task which is still far from complete, and only a small part of them has so far been published. Much investigation was also necessary before the possibility of the automatists having obtained the information by any normal means could be ruled out. Notable among those who undertook this work were the second Lord Balfour, Sir Oliver Lodge, J. G. Piddington, Mrs. Henry Sidgwick and Miss Alice Johnson.

From the scripts it appears as if Myers, together with Edmund Gurney (died 1888) and Henry Sidgwick (died 1900), devised these cross-correspondences as a watertight means of demonstrating their survival. The communicator purporting to be Myers wrote for example through Mrs. Piper, "I am trying with all the forces . . . together to prove that I am Myers," and through Mrs. Holland, "Oh, I am feeble with eagerness—how can I best be identified." There are also many references to the method employed. Thus in Mrs. Verrall's script appears, "Record the bits and when fitted they will make the whole," and in Mrs. Willett's, "That I have different scribes means that I must show different aspects of thoughts underlying which unity is found," and, "I know what Lodge wants. He wants me to prove that I have access to knowledge shown elsewhere." An early script of Mrs. Holland's gives a description of the conditions the communicator is working in: "The nearest simile I can find to express the difficulties of sending a message—is that I appear to be standing behind a sheet of frosted glass which blurs sight and deadens sound—dictating feebly to a reluctant and somewhat obtuse secretary."

The cross-correspondences are so complex, so allusive, and depend so often on an extremely close acquaintance with English and classical literature as on the personal circumstances of the group, that it is impossible to summarize adequately even one of them in the space available here. I have tried in this book to present in each case enough evidence to enable readers to judge for themselves, but they must take my word that this would not give a fair impression of the cross-correspondences. Many of the references are so subtle that considerable research was needed to unearth them, and even now a number have probably been overlooked. A very just and readable account of the cross-correspondences is given by H. F. Saltmarsh in *Evidence of Personal Survival from Cross Correspondences.*[6] To demonstrate the method involved Saltmarsh invented the following fictitious example:

"Suppose that the topic chosen was 'Time.' Automatist A might start the ball rolling by a quotation from the hymn, 'Like an ever-rolling stream.' Automatist B might follow on with a quotation from *Alice in Wonderland* dealing with the discussion concerning Time at the Mad Hatter's tea-table, e.g. 'He won't stand beating,' or, 'We quarrelled last March—just before he went mad, you know' and then, Automatist C gives the clue with 'Time and tide wait for no man.' If the investigator were to recognize the source of these quotations, he would see that there was a common idea in all of them, viz., Time."

Saltmarsh weighs up the possibilities as follows:

First, in view of the enormous number of detailed cross-correspondence in the scripts and of the explicit statements that these are parts of a planned experiment, he concludes that "the chance hypothesis has very little to recommend it, though it is, of course, abstractly possible."

Second, in view of the precautions taken, of the character of those involved, and of the thirty years over which the scripts spread, he considers "the hypothesis of fraud is so fantastic that it need only be mentioned to be dismissed."

If these two hypotheses are dismissed, we seem left with some form of ESP as the explanation of the cross-correspondences. The final question is therefore whether they can be adequately explained by clairvoyance and telepathy between the living, or whether we should accept them as the evidence of survival they purport to be. In the simpler cross-references, ESP between the living can, Saltmarsh concludes, provide an entirely satisfactory explanation, but "in my opinion we soon reach a point where the hypotheses of simple telepathy and clairvoyance become so strained that they are untenable"; if we are to stick to the explanation of ESP between the living we are driven to postulate "telepathy between the automatists and/or the investigators, combined with subliminal in excess of supraliminal knowledge."

In his scrupulously fair-minded summary Saltmarsh comes to no final conclusion as between this hypothesis and the alternative that the cross-correspondences were in fact inspired in some way by the surviving personalities of Myers and his group. While accepting either hypothesis as tenable, my own feeling is that the cross-correspondences provide the best evidence of survival known to us. While either hypothesis is undeniably tenable, it may be hoped that when we know more about "normal" ESP and its mode of operation, we shall be able to judge the probabilities more accurately.

Such cases as I have described in this chapter seem to many people to provide strong evidence of survival. Some parapsychologists believe, however, that they can be explained by clairvoyance or by telepathy from the living, or by a combination of the two: Zorab's criticism of the Chaffin Will case is in point. It is certainly true that much information obtained through mediums can be explained in this way, as the famous "Gordon Davis" case strikingly illustrates. This case, reported by Dr. S. G. Soal,[7] has been frequently quoted, but it is so important that it cannot be omitted here.

During a sitting in January, 1922, with Mrs. Blanche Cooper, a well-known British medium, Dr. Soal received a message from a "communicator" claiming to be the spirit of a boyhood friend named Gordon Davis, whom Soal believed to have been killed some years before. "Davis" described, correctly and in some detail, a number of events that had occurred during their school days, and the circumstances in which they had last met. At a subsequent sitting, the same medium gave a detailed description of the house where Davis had supposedly lived since they last met. This description contained particulars not only of the layout of the house, but also of the disposition of various items in it.

Soal made copious notes, which proved fortunate, for three years later, in April, 1925, he discovered that Davis was still living and was in business as an estate agent at Southend. He visited him, and was astonished to find that the house corresponded exactly with the description given by the medium. Not a single statement she had made was wrong, and her many correct ones included the following:

A dark tunnel ran through the house into the back garden.

There was a "verandah" (a seaside shelter) opposite.

The name of the street in which the house stood began with two E's (it was Eastern Esplanade).

The pictures on the walls were of mountains and sea, with one of them depicting a road between two hills.

There was a black bird on the piano (this was an ornamental king-fisher).

There were two "funny saucers" on the walls, and there were some curious vases.

There were two brass candlesticks downstairs.

A woman and a child were in the house (Mrs. Davis had a young son).

Here, some kind of ESP seems clearly to have been at work: Dr. Soal calculated that the odds were several million to one against such a combination of details fitting a town house chosen at random. The most interesting feature of the case is that in 1922, at the time of the sitting, the Davis family was living in London and the furniture was in storage, and they did not move to the house at Southend until some months after the date of the sitting.

Telepathy alone, therefore, cannot explain the medium's statements, and we seem obliged to conclude that precognition must have been involved.

Another case, casting similar doubt on the validity of many so-called proofs of survival, is that reported by Canon Douglas. He had a chauffeur, a Frenchman named Réallier, who during the first world war returned to his homeland to join the French army. Some years later, at a sitting with a medium, Réallier "came through." A deceased nephew of the Canon, also correctly named, purported to be assisting Réallier to communicate. Much evidential matter concerning both was given, some of which the Canon knew at the time to be true, and some of which he was able to confirm later. As with Gordon Davis, however, it was subsequently established that the chauffeur was still alive, and had never been near death or even critically ill.[8]

The cases of Gordon Davis and Réallier cannot, of course, in themselves render valueless the apparently convincing indications of survival mentioned earlier in this chapter; but they do illustrate the need for scrupulous caution in considering such indications. Some investigators, aware of this difficulty, have tried to tackle the problem another way, leaving sealed packages whose contents, known only to themselves, they would endeavour to communicate after death. Myers and Lodge were two who attempted this. Most purported communications by them proved inconclusive, but at least two mediums received "communications" allegedly from Lodge which certainly achieved very close descriptions of the package he had deposited, as was proven when this was finally opened. Such knowledge need not have derived from Lodge's surviving mind, however, but might well have been obtained by clairvoyance. Since the sealed package in experiments of this kind must ultimately be opened to check the validity of supposed communications, it is clearly also possible that a medium could learn its contents through precognition. Experiments on these lines can thus never provide convincing proof of survival.

It was in order to overcome the limitations of such attempts to demonstrate survival that Professor R. H. Thouless devised a more complex type of test. Its basis is an encyphered passage, supposedly impossible to break without a key-word which is to be communicated after death. The value of this test lies not only in the fact that one word would presumably be easier for the deceased communicator to remember than a lengthy message, but, more important, in the fact that any number of unsuccessful attempts may be made without spoiling the test—as happens when a sealed envelope is opened for checking. A vital requirement of the test is, as Thouless states, "that attempts should be made while I am still alive to obtain the key through mediums. If there have been a sufficient number of such attempts during my life and all have been unsuccessful while an equal or smaller number of attempts after my death have led to success, the conclusion that the key has been supplied by me as a still existing communicator and not through a retrocognitive process of the medium or sitters will be very strongly indicated." This test cannot, of course, be completed until after Professor Thouless's death, which his well-wishers trust may be long postponed. It is therefore to be hoped that many other interested enquirers may adopt a similar experiment, which seems to provide the opportunity for a highly convincing proof of survival.[9]

Clearly, the position is by no means easy or clear-cut. It is, I think, well-put by Professor Gardner Murphy:

"Often a more appropriate attitude in science than belief or disbelief is to say: 'It would be sheer chicanery to pretend that I have a right to an opinion.' This is a point of view which may properly have a strong claim upon our allegiance in psychical research. We may well respect those who, like Drayton Thomas, have reached an honest conclusion in favor of full survival of personality after death, or those who, like Professor Dodds, wholeheartedly reject the hypothesis. But another position which is fully as defensible at the present time is that of saying that the case rests upon dead center, waiting for evidence *so good,* or objections *so sound,* as to warrant forming a judgment."[10]

REFERENCES

1. Myers, F. W. H.: *Human Personality and its Survival of Bodily Death.* London, 1903.
2. Case of the Will of Mr. James L. Chaffin, *Proc. SPR, 36*:517-24.
3. Zorab, George: Cases of the Chaffin Will type and the problem of survival, *Journ. SPR, 41*:407-417.
4. Lodge, Oliver J.: *Raymond Revised.* London, 1922.
5. Dingwall, E. J., and Langdon-Davies, J.: *The Unknown — Is it Nearer?* New York, 1956.

6. Saltmarsh, H. F.: *Evidence of Personal Survival from Cross Corre-spondences.* London, 1938.

7. Soal, S. G.: A report on some communications received through Mrs. Blanche Cooper, *Proc. SPR, 35*:471-594.

8. Murphy, Gardner: Difficulties confronting the survival hypothe-sis, *Journ. ASPR, 39*:67-94.

9. Thouless, R. H.: A test of survival, *Proc. SPR, 48*:253-263.

10. Murphy, Gardner: *loc. cit.*

Chapter 9

MODERN EXPERIMENTAL PARAPSYCHOLOGY

*"Parapsychology is the science dealing with those biological
or psychological events which show that the categories
of matter, space and time (and thus of causality)
are not axiomatic."*

C. G. Jung

Modern experimental parapsychology is generally accepted as
dating from 1930, when Dr. J. B. Rhine began his famous experiments. His work first became widely known in 1934, when he
published an account of it in a book, *Extra-Sensory Perception*: a
term, incidentally, which Dr. Rhine originated.

Rhine's work differed from that of his predecessors in one
important respect. It was the first large-scale programme of *quantitative* experiments, in which the results could be assessed mathematically. The advantages of such experiments had long been
recognized; indeed, as early as 1885, Sir Oliver Lodge had suggested
their use in tests for telepathy, and had given a mathematical formula for assessing the results. What work of this kind had been
done, such as that of Coover and Estabrooks which I mentioned
earlier, was, however, on far too small a scale to provide reliable
information.

In most of his experiments, Rhine employed card-guessing
techniques using special packs of "Zener" cards, each consisting of
five sets of five cards bearing one of five simple patterns; a circle,
a cross, a star, a square or three wavy lines. The subject would be
asked to guess as each card was turned up from a shuffled pack.
If no other factor but chance were involved, obviously an average
of five correct calls for each "run" of twenty-five cards could be
expected, so that the presence of some factor other than chance
could be inferred if a subject continued to score substantially more
(or less) than five over a series of runs.

Rhine was fortunate in having plenty of subjects, in the form of students, to hand, and with many of those tested it soon became clear that something more than mere chance was involved. Some maintained, over thousands of calls, average scores of more than double those attributable to chance. With a few "star" subjects the odds against chance were literally astronomical. One, at a first attempt, correctly guessed nine successive cards in a run of twenty-five—against odds of two million to one—and the next day he did exactly the same thing again. Another, a girl of twelve, once guessed the whole pack correctly in one run. Here the odds against chance are more than 600,000,000,000,000 to one.

With the publication of *Extra-Sensory Perception* Dr. Rhine became the target of a great deal of criticism, particularly from the ranks of the more orthodox psychologists. Much of it was ill-founded and some downright abusive, and considerable emotionalism was evident among Rhine's supporters as well as his detractors. It was argued by many that Rhine's statistical calculations must in some way be invalid, but this claim was clearly refuted by independent statisticians. One of them, J. A. Greenwood, compared 2,500 calls which had been made in past ESP tests with the order in which cards were turned up in no less than two hundred newly shuffled packs. He found that the "score" obtained in this way conformed closely to theoretical chance expectation.[1]

Further corroboration was unintentionally provided by one of Rhine's critics, an American conjuror named Mulholland, who was so certain the results were lucky flukes that he commissioned the International Business Machines Corporation to feed thousands of cards into a machine which automatically shuffled them and delivered them in pairs. Contrary to Mulholland's expectations these results also conformed closely to theoretical probability. Mulholland presented his findings in such a misleading way that at first sight there appeared to be significant deviations from the theoretical chance average. The fallaciousness of Mulholland's criticism, and the fact that his experiment really demonstrates the opposite, have been clearly shown by Dr. D. J. West.[2]

Attempts to repeat Dr. Rhine's successes were made by other experimenters, notably Dr. S. G. Soal, a professional mathematician and a well-known psychical researcher. Soal followed the methods introduced by Rhine, but took even stricter precautions against the possibility of cheating or the use (deliberately or unconsciously) of sensory clues. Although initially sceptical, Dr. Soal applied himself to his task with great tenacity. Over a period of five years he tested more than 150 subjects and recorded over 120,000 guesses—all, it seemed, capable of explanation by the laws of chance. He also tested the well-known medium Mrs. Eileen Garrett, with whom Dr. Rhine had achieved striking results, but with no better success. Not surprisingly, Dr. Soal began to wonder what magical ingredient enabled ESP to work in America but not in Britain, and whether there could be any undiscovered flaw in Rhine's methods.

Then came a breakthrough. The British parapsychologist W. Whately Carington, who was conducting some telepathy experiments at the time, reported to Soal that in some cases he had observed a *displacement effect*—that certain subjects seemed to score, not on the "target" of the moment, but on either that which had preceded it or that *which was to follow*. He urged Soal to check his results for this effect, and when this was done two subjects were found to have been scoring well above chance in both directions.

These subjects were Mr. Basil Shackleton, a photographer, and Mrs. Gloria Stewart, the wife of a consulting engineer. Analysis showed that Mrs. Stewart had guessed which card was to follow 457 times as against a chance expectation of 384 times. The odds against chance here work out at more than 1,000,000 to one. Shackleton's scores showed similarly significant results. None of Dr. Soal's other subjects showed any ability of this kind.

In the light of these findings a further series of experiments was conducted under stringent conditions, this time in collaboration with Mrs. K. M. Goldney, a prominent member of the SPR. These took place over the period 1941-3. Particular precautions were taken to ensure that any results would indicate true precognition and not telepathy. To this end a list of random numbers (one to five) was compiled from a table of logarithms and from published tables of random numbers. These were written down on scoring sheets in columns of twenty-five so that a guess could be recorded against each. It was thus ensured that the order of the numbers was not the result of some pre-existing pattern in Soal's mind. Instead of a Zener pack, five single picture cards were used, each portraying an animal—elephant, giraffe, lion, pelican and zebra.

The experiments took place in two rooms, one opening from the other. In the larger of these the person acting as "agent" sat at a table facing Mrs. Goldney, but separated from her by a screen with a small hole in it. In the other sat the "percipient," Shackleton, with Dr. Soal. The door was left slightly ajar so that the experimenters could signal when they were ready, but the seating was so arranged that it was impossible to see from one table to the other. As a further precaution the cards were placed in a box having only the side nearest the agent open. The outer door of the rooms was locked during the experiments.

Before each run of fifty trials the five picture cards were shuffled and laid in a row in the agent's box face downwards. A scoring sheet, hitherto seen by no one but Dr. Soal, was handed to Mrs. Goldney, who also had five cards in front of her, numbered from one to five. For each trial she held up to the hole in the screen the card bearing the number indicated on the scoring sheet. The agent then picked up the corresponding picture card from the row in his box, looked at it and replaced it. At a call from Mrs. Goldney the percipient wrote down the initial letter of the animal of his guess on a blank scoring sheet. No conversation other than the "call" was permitted. After each run the picture cards were turned up to see which animal corresponded to each number card. The appropriate numbers were then filled in on the percipient's score sheet and compared with those on the sheet used by Mrs. Goldney.

Analysis of Shackleton's results showed that by far the highest scores he attained were on the card that the agent was to look at in the *next call ahead*. During 1941, he guessed the future card 1,101 times in 3,789 trials, 325 times more than the theoretical chance expectation, the odds against chance being ten million, million, million, million, million, million to one.

Carington's experiments, which led Soal to resume his own, were designed as tests of telepathy. His techniques differed from Rhine's in several respects. Any number of subjects could take part simultaneously and they were able to remain in their own homes, or indeed, be anywhere and still take part. Carington avoided card guessing, which he thought conducive to boredom and thus likely to inhibit results. Instead he used drawings of easily identified objects, which he selected by an ingenious method. He first opened a book of mathematical tables at random and noted the last digits of the first three or four entries on the page. Then he opened a dictionary at the page indicated by the number thus obtained, and selected the first suitable item on that page. The percipients knew nothing more than that the targets were easily drawn objects.

Carington would then make a drawing of the object and pin it up in his study, where it remained from early evening until the next morning. It was then locked away. During the period of exposure Carington's study was kept locked, and heavy curtains ensured that no one could see into the room. The percipients were provided with special forms on which they drew whatever came into their minds during the period concerned. Each was supplied with a photograph of the study, and this, Carington believed, stimulated interest and assisted the telepathic process. Each experiment covered a period of ten days. The drawings were sent to Carington, who marked each with a reference number indicating the percipient and the target picture displayed when it was made. They were then passed to an independent judge who compared them with the target pictures and decided whether any resemblances existed. The judge did not know which drawing had been aimed at any particular target, but made his assessment purely on resemblances.

Subsequent analysis showed clear evidence of an ESP effect; it also showed that this effect was not merely confined to the target aimed at on a given day, but was spread over the whole ten days. The number of hits on a particular target gradually increased on the days preceding that on which it was displayed, and declined in the same manner afterwards. This "scattering" or "clustering" effect was not only a displacement in time, but the forward displacement demonstrated true precognition, for the targets concerned had not then been selected.

The clustering effect noted by Carington is not always a feature of displacement, however. For instance, Dr. C. E. Stuart, in some experiments with similar drawings at Duke University, found that certain subjects consistently scored either on the target next ahead or the one last behind according to whether the test was for clairvoyance or for telepathy. This was also largely true in the case of Dr. Soal's subject Shackleton.

The validity of the results of experiments such as those outlined above has often been criticized on the grounds that the selection of targets may be influenced by an unconscious bias on the part of the experimenters or a preference for certain symbols by the subjects. To overcome this criticism various kinds of mechanical, and more recently electronic, "randomizers" have been developed. The first modern parapsychologist to use such a device was a contemporary of Carington's, G. N. M. Tyrrell.

Unlike most workers who devise an experiment and then find suitable subjects to test, Tyrrell designed his most important experiments around one particular subject. This subject, Miss G. M. Johnson, seemed to have a remarkable ability for finding missing objects, and Tyrrell's aim was to take the fullest advantage of this faculty. His apparatus was developed as the experiments progressed.

Initially it consisted of a row of five small boxes with hinged lids mounted against a wooden screen, with a hole through the screen into each box through which the experimenter could insert a pointer forming the target. The subject was required to lift the lid of the box into which she believed the pointer had been thrust. Chance expectation of a correct guess was, of course, one in five. Highly significant scores were obtained in this way.

Tyrrell next elaborated his apparatus by substituting electric lamps for the pointer. To record her guess the subject pressed a button which caused the lamp in the appropriate box to light up. Scores obtained in this way were automatically recorded on a paper tape. They too were highly significant.

A further refinement was the provision of a switch which changed over the connections from buttons to lamps in such a way that the subject could not know which lamp she was lighting. An even more interesting modification was the introduction of a relay giving a time delay and switches operated by the lids of the boxes. The subject had to raise the lid of the box containing the lamp she thought would light up after she had done so. By using the change-over switch, the experimenter could prevent himself from knowing which it was to be, thus eliminating the possibility of telepathy. Scoring with this method was as high as with the others.

During this time, the Parapsychology Laboratory at Duke University continued to develop, and Dr. Rhine and his colleagues issued a number of impressive reports. Outstanding among these was the account of an experiment carried out in 1933-34 by Dr. J. G. Pratt with a "star" subject, Hubert Pearce. This experiment, designed as a test for clairvoyance, was conducted with the experimenter and the subject in different buildings more than one hundred yards apart. At a prearranged time, Dr. Pratt laid the top card of a shuffled pack of Zener cards face down on the table. He continued in this way at one minute intervals until he had gone through two packs, then turned them over and made a written record of their order. At the same time, Pearce made a similar record of his guesses. Pratt did not see Pearce until both had handed copies of their records to Dr. Rhine for checking. Over a series of fifteen experiments Pearce averaged nearly nine hits per run of twenty-five cards, representing odds against chance of more than a hundred million, million, million to one.

Drs. Rhine and Pratt regard the "Pearce-Pratt Series" as "the first experiment which in our judgment met the criteria for a conclusive test of ESP."[3] These standards of control have been maintained and are taken for granted in all serious modern ESP experiments.

In 1943, Rhine exploded his second bombshell. He published a report in which he claimed that significant results had been obtained in experiments involving pyschokinesis, the direct effect of mind upon matter.

Rhine began his investigations into psychokinesis by testing the claims of a "crap-shooter" who believed he could "will" dice to fall with certain faces uppermost. He used methods of scoring similar to those developed in his ESP experiments, and the odds against chance were calculated in the same way. Various developments in technique were made to meet criticisms of the first experiments: these included mechanical methods of throwing, and specially balanced and calibrated dice. Dr. Rhine's results have led him to claim that "a good case has been made for the occurrence of PK as an aspect of psi." It is generally considered, however, that the evidence for PK is not nearly as strong as for ESP.

In 1951-2, G. W. Fisk, editor of the *Journal* and *Proceedings* of the SPR, and A. M. J. Mitchell carried out a series of combined ESP-PK tests. Fisk displayed a target, determined from tables of random numbers and changed daily, at his home. The subjects, in their respective homes, had to throw dice and will them to fall in a way that produced a score corresponding to the target displayed at the time. Thus they had to find out the target by ESP and aim at it by PK. Of ten subjects four scored slightly above chance expectation, while one, Dr. Jessie Blundun, produced, during 10,000 trials, a score with odds against chance expectation of more than 30,000 to one.

Fisk used Dr. Blundun in further experiments made in collaboration with Dr. Donald J. West. Various refinements in technique were introduced and meticulous analyses made of the results. Although Dr. Blundun did not approach the remarkable results of the first experiments she continued to produce scores significantly above chance expectation. Dr. Blundun's home was some 200 miles from Fisk's, and her only contact with him during the experiments was by correspondence.[4]

In both ESP and PK experiments, it is common to find that the highest scores are made early in a series of trials and gradually fall away. This is not always so, however. Some subjects tend to show high scores at the beginning and ending of a run; others produce their best results in the middle. A variety of other effects have been noted in individual cases.

This "decline effect" was at first thought to be due to fatigue, but this view is not now held by most parapsychologists. It was through the study of decline effects that Rhine made another important discovery. He found that when he made a subject continue to make calls without a break over a long period the scoring, after falling to the level of chance expectation, continued to decline until it became significantly *negative*. Such scores are just as much evidence of ESP as positive ones: indeed, to produce equivalent odds against chance it is necessary to misname a much greater number of cards. It was found that some subjects were able to produce negative instead of positive scores upon request, while others could only produce one or the other.

Attempts to establish whether any relationship exists between the type of scoring—negative or positive—and the attitude and psychological background of the subject have been made by a number of workers, notably Dr. Gertrude R. Schmeidler, an American psychologist. Dr. Schmeidler divided her subjects into two categories, "sheep" and "goats." Sheep were people who accepted "the possibility of paranormal success in the given experimental situation," even if they were not sure that they themselves would succeed. Goats were subjects who believed there was "no possibility of paranormal success in the given experimental situation," even if they believed that in other circumstances paranormal success might occur.

Over the period 1943-51, Dr. Schmeidler collected, from groups and individual subjects, a total of nearly 300,000 guesses at ESP cards. Most of the tests were for clairvoyance, with the targets hidden from both experimenters and subjects when the guesses were made, but some, in which an agent looked at each card, were general ESP tests where results might be attributable to telepathy or clairvoyance (GESP). Analysis showed significant scores in both directions and although they were small—about four per cent difference from chance expectation—they indicated that sheep tended to score consistently above chance, while goats gave equally consistent negative scores.

Dr. Schmeidler took her investigation a stage further by applying a standard psychological test, the Rorschach, to more than 1,000 subjects. The Rorschach personality test is applied by showing the subject ten standard ink blots, in themselves meaningless, and asking him to state what they look like or what they remind him of. In this case the test was used to distinguish between subjects who were well adjusted socially and those who were not. Results showed that significant scoring by both sheep and goats was confined almost entirely to subjects who were well adjusted socially.[5]

A similar line of research has been followed by Dr. Betty

Humphrey, a colleague of Dr. Rhine at Duke University, using various psychological tests, particularly the "expansion-compression" drawing test devised by Paula Elkisch. In this test the subject draws whatever he pleases and is classed as expansive or compressive according to the type of drawing he produces. Clear, bold drawings that fill the paper and make the fullest use of whatever artistic ability the subject posseses are normally associated with expansive types, whereas cramped, feeble and uncertain pictures are typical of compressive types. They correspond roughly to Jung's classification of extroverts and introverts. Dr. Humphrey found that in clairvoyance tests although all the subjects were consciously aiming for high scores only the expansive types tended to produce them. The compressive types tended to give negative scores. In telepathy or GESP tests when an agent looked at the cards, however, the position was reversed, the compressive types tending to score significantly above chance and the expansive types below.[6]

Much of the more recent experimental work in parapsychology has been concerned with the establishment of the psychological factors involved in the occurrence of psi phenomena. It has been established that one such factor is novelty or spontaneity in the experimental conditions. At Duke University, Pratt and Woodruff studied the effect of variations in the size of ESP cards. They found that although scores were not influenced by the actual size of the Zener packs used, a sudden change from large to small packs, or *vice versa,* produced a measurable rise in the scoring level.[7] The effect of spontaneity was also demonstrated at Duke by Scherer, using colored balls instead of cards.[8]

The result of an experiment by Fisk and West shows that the emotional content of symbols used in a test can also influence scoring. Fisk observed that a certain subject tested with Zener cards showed a preference in his calls for the cross and circle. The subject explained that these two symbols were emotionally significant for him because he associated them with the male and female genital organs. Fisk prepared a special Zener pack in which the cross and circle cards had erotic pictures (cut from *La Vie Parisienne* and similar magazines) covering them. Fisk, acting as agent, used this special pack for the first few runs but afterwards used a normal

pack and simply recalled in his mind the appropriate picture whenever a cross or a circle was turned up. The subject had copies of
the pictures before him, and was not told when Fisk was using only
the normal symbol cards. Scores obtained in this experiment were
significantly above chance expectation.[9]

The attitude of both experimenter and subject, not only towards ESP, but towards each other, has long been regarded as an
important factor. Soal noted this in his work with Shackleton and
Mrs. Stewart, and Carington also attached great importance to it.
Confirmatory evidence is provided by the work of two Americans,
Margaret Anderson and Rhea White, who studied the effect of
pupil-teacher attitudes on the results of clairvoyance tests. In their
first study, made with elementary and high school children whose
teachers acted as agents, they found that pupils who liked their
teacher scored significantly high, whereas those who expressed a
dislike gave significantly low scores. A later study showed that the
highest scores were made by children who both liked and were
liked by their teacher, and the lowest by those who disliked and
were disliked by the teacher. The Anderson-White studies also
indicate that age is not an important factor in the success of children at ESP tests.[10]

One of the chief difficulties in psi research is in devising experiments that are repeatable. In general, the tests producing the
most outstanding results are those made with specially gifted "star"
subjects, and cannot, therefore, be repeated exactly by others. For
this reason, group tests such as those with school children and students are of particular value. Another aid to repeatability is the
use of mechanical and electronic methods of randomizing and scoring. These techniques were employed in a successful experiment
by S. D. Kahn and U. A. Neisser at Harvard in 1949-50.

In this experiment the randomizing, counting and checking
were done mechanically by the IBM Corporation. Instead of guessing at cards, the subjects were required to make a pencil mark for
each call in one of five spaces on a special form. The experimenter
used a similar form and marked his targets on it from a list of random numbers. Both forms were afterwards fed into a machine
which worked out the scores automatically. In the course of the

experiment, more than 100 subjects between them recorded 43,278 guesses. A significant overall score resulted, with odds against chance of approximately 2,000 to one. Distances ranging from half a mile to 500 miles separated the subjects from the targets, the scoring of those at the greatest distance being slightly higher than that of those nearest the targets.[11]

These results by Kahn and Neisser were exceptional. Most mass ESP experiments have failed to produce significant results. In a test carried out via the medium of television by Donald Michie and D. J. West, only one person out of 1,367 who sent in their guesses achieved an outstanding score, and no generalized ESP effect was noted.[12] A large-scale experiment organized by R. G. Medhurst, H. Stark and G. T. Thompson in 1961-62, in the hope of finding àn outstanding subject, was similarly abortive.

Medhurst's subjects, recruited through letters published in the British national press, made preliminary tests in their homes with ordinary playing cards and sent scores to Medhurst and his colleagues for checking. The test consisted of 400 guesses, made under either "telepathic" or "clairvoyant" conditions, as the subject chose. (A preference was shown for the "clairvoyance" test.) Subjects who scored at a high significance level in the first tests were retested under supervision. Those whose initial scores were marginal were given a second unsupervised test and, if the total score of the two reached significant level, subsequently given a supervised test. About 2,500 people volunteered and 1,200 completed score sheets were sent in. About thirty subjects carried out supervised tests, some of them being visited repeatedly. Medhurst reports that "while a few initially achieved witnessed scores of marginal significance, none has been able to produce clearly significant results under adequate conditions. No Basil Shackletons have emerged!"[13]

Attempts have been made to develop or enhance ESP performance by various means. The use of hypnosis is discussed in Chapter Six. The use of drugs is another method for which success has been claimed. The outstanding work of Brugmans, who tested the effect of bromide and alcohol on the subject van Dam, has already been mentioned: Brugmans, it will be remembered, found that these drugs produced a significant increase in scoring. Rhine has noted that in both ESP and PK tests the effect of narcotic drugs in heavy doses has been to interfere with positive scoring and produce chance results.[14] R. J. Cadoret found that in tests with ESP cards, sodium amytal, a sedative, caused a limited decline in scoring, and dexadrine, a stimulant, caused a significant fall. In tests with free response material, however, while sodium amytal still produced a decline, dexadrine caused an improvement in scoring.[15] Pamela M. Huby and C. W. M. Wilson, who recently conducted some experiments on the effects of a variety of drugs, were unable to repeat Cadoret's results.[16]

Insufficient has been done for any conclusions yet to be reached on the effect of drugs on ESP or PK, although it seems that in general large doses of narcotics do affect results. This is not surprising in view of the known effect of these drugs, and there is little evidence of any direct effect upon the psi capacity itself.

Another question, which is currently receiving the attention of parapsychologists, is the relation of psi to the functioning of the nervous system. Particular interest is centered upon experiments involving the use of the electro-encephalograph, an instrument which records the electrical activity of the brain. Potential differences between electrodes placed on the scalp are amplified to an intensity sufficient to activate oscillograph pens which trace records on a moving paper strip. The resulting record is termed an electro-encephalogram (EEG). For a brief explanation of its principle of operation the following, by Edward Osborn, would be difficult to improve upon:

"The electrical activity of the cortex consists of more or less continuous rhythmic fluctuations of potential. In normal adults, awake, relaxed, and with eyes closed, the brain rhythm, in the absence of specific stimulation, ranges in frequency from 8 to 13 cycles per second, with an average of about 10 c/s., while the amplitude may fluctuate spontaneously. Both frequency and amplitude vary from individual to individual, and to some extent within the E.E.G. of a single individual. This rhythm, which is known as the alpha rhythm, is suppressed by attention or perception. During the process of going to sleep, marked changes occur in the E.E.G.

The various stages may be described in general terms as follows: (a) relaxed and resting, but awake—normal alpha rhythm, followed by diminution of amplitude; (b) drowsy, entering the stage of light sleep—the alpha rhythm fades away and short spindles of faster activity often appear, followed by slow waves of 4 to 5 c/s.; (c) real sleep—spindle-shaped bursts of waves, about 14 c/s., appear, and slow waves increase in magnitude and decrease in frequency; (d) deep sleep—spindles disappear, and slow waves become very large and very slow, less than 1 c/s."[17]

Osborn (whose untimely death, in 1957, was a great blow to the SPR—he was editor of its *Proceedings* and *Journal*) gave that description in his introduction to a report on an EEG experiment with Mrs. Eileen J. Garrett. This experiment, designed to show any difference in various states—normal consciousness, hypnosis, mediumistic trance, etc.—proved largely negative.

A number of quantitative EEG experiments have also been made, notably by the Research Committee of the ASPR,[18] S. C. Wallwork[19] and Charles C. Tart.[20] Here again, results were disappointing.

The use of the electro-encephalograph in this manner is a development of more simple techniques also designed to determine whether psi activity is accompanied by physiological changes. J. Hettinger[21] measured the galvanic skin responses of subjects and noted significant changes when agents, located at distances of up to 200 miles, were subjected to stimuli such as noises and physical exertion.

Dr. Stepán Figar,[22] a Czech, seems to have had remarkable success in telepathy experiments using the plethysmograph, an instrument which records changes in the volume of the fingertips resulting from contraction or dilation of the peripheral blood-vessels. These changes are known to coincide with emotional and mental reactions. As with the EEG, plethysmograms are recorded on a moving band of paper. Figar took plethysmograms of agent and subject simultaneously, and in many cases found that stimuli applied to the agent produced strikingly similar responses by both. This was particularly evident when agent and subject were related, and outstandingly so in one test with a mother and son. It will be noted that, unlike most telepathy tests, no communication of ideas or tangible information was involved. So far as I am aware no one has yet repeated Figar's experiments and confirmed his results.

Clearly, it is impossible in a single chapter, or for that matter in one book, to give more than a cursory outline of the way in which modern experimental parapsychology has developed and is proceeding. My aim here has been to draw a broad and general picture, giving sufficient references to facilitate further study.

REFERENCES

1. Greenwood, J. A.: Analysis of a large chance control series, *Journ. Parapsychology*, 2:138-146.
2. West, D. J.: *Psychical Research Today*. London, 1962.
3. Rhine, J. B., and Pratt, J. G.: *Parapsychology, Frontier Science of the Mind*. Springfield, 1958.
4. Fisk, G. W., and West, D. J.: Dice-casting experiments with a single subject, *Journ. SPR, 39*: 697:277-87.
5. Schmeidler, Gertrude: *ESP in Relation to Rorschach Test Evaluation*. New York, 1960.
6. Humphrey, Betty M.: The relation of ESP to mode of drawing, *Journ. Parapsychology*, 13:31-46.
7. Pratt, J. G., and Woodruff, J. L.: Size of stimulus symbols in extrasensory perception, *Journ. Parapsychology*, 3:121-58.
8. Scherer, W. B.: Spontaneity as a factor in ESP, *Journ. Parapsychology*, 12:126-147.
9. Fisk, G. W., and West, D. J.: ESP tests with erotic symbols, *Journ. SPR, 38*: 683:1-7.
10. Anderson, Margaret, and White, Rhea: Teacher-pupil attitudes and clairvoyance test results, *Journ. Parapsychology,* 20:141-157.
11. Kahn, S. D.: Studies in extrasensory perception: experiments utilizing an electric scoring device, *Proc. ASPR, 25*:1-48.
12. West, D. J.: *op. cit.*
13. Medhurst, R. G.: Personal communication to the author.
14. Rhine, J. B., and Pratt, J. G.: *op. cit.*
15. Cadoret, R. J.: The effect of Amytal and Dexedrine on ESP performance, *Journ. Parapsychology*, 17:259-74.
16. Huby, Pamela M., and Wilson, C. W. M.: The effect of drugs on ESP ability, *Journ. SPR, 41*: 708:60-67.

17. Evans, C. C., and Osborn, Edward: An experiment in the electro-encephalography of mediumistic trances, *Journ. SPR, 36*: 669: 588-596.

18. American Society for Psychical Research, Research Committee, Report for 1958. *Journ. ASPR, 53*: 2:69-71.

19. Wallwork, S. C.: ESP experiments with simultaneous electro-encephalographic recordings, *Journ. SPR, 36*: 672:697-701.

20. Tart, Charles C.: Physiological correlates of psi cognition, *International Journ. Parapsychology, 5*: 4:375-386.

21. Hettinger, J.: *Telepathy and Spiritualism.* New York, 1952.

22. Figar, Stepán: The application of plethysmography to the objective study of so-called extrasensory perception, *Journ. SPR, 40*: 702:162-702.

Chapter 10

PSYCHOLOGICAL ELEMENTS IN TESTIMONY

"Do me eyes deceive me earsight?"
(Artemus Ward His Book)
CHARLES FARRAR BROWNE

IN CONSIDERING apparently paranormal happenings, observers who are unaccustomed to weighing evidence usually assume there are two main alternatives: either that deliberate deception has taken place, or that the phenomena are genuinely paranormal. In this chapter I want to illustrate the fallacy behind such an assumption, and to indicate what a wide range of claimed phenomena can frequently be explained as arising from mal-observation, self-delusion, preconceived ideas, and other human weaknesses, without any imputation of fraud or bad faith. The professional investigator's scrupulous sifting of evidence has often been misunderstood as conveying such imputations, when in fact it is a necessary consequence of his awareness of human fallibility; and the resentment and heightened emotionalism engendered by such misunderstanding themselves form a further barrier in arriving at the truth. It is important, therefore, to establish the criteria by which the testimony of witnesses is to be judged.

The law, in its examination of witnesses, has long recognized the psychological elements that must be taken into account. In one of the leading legal authorities on evidence, Archbold, the position is stated thus:

"Although a witness is perfectly disinterested, although he is a man of integrity and veracity, and has a just sense of the moral obligation of the oath he has taken, still the degree of credit to be given to his testimony depends upon his real knowledge of the facts to which he testifies. A man may be deceived in a fact, from deriving his knowledge of it through a false medium; from defects in his power of observation; from his attention being occupied more by the circumstances accompanying it than by the fact itself at the time of its occurrence; or from a thousand other circumstances, which, if candidly stated, might be satisfactorily answered and accounted for by the other party, so as to convince the witness himself that he laboured under a mistake. Where there is a doubt, therefore, whether the evidence given by a witness is not founded on some misconception, it is the duty of the counsel who cross-examine him to question him as to the sources of his knowledge; his reasons for believing the fact to be as he has stated, his reasons for recollecting it; the circumstances attending its occurrence; whether it was light or dark; and whether he was near or distant at the time it occurred, and the like; so that the jury may be able to judge of the degree of confidence they should place in the witness's testimony. If a witness refuses to answer such questions, or does not answer them satisfactorily, it should have the effect of detracting considerably from his credit in the estimation of the jury."[1]

Such fallibility is well known to psychologists, and was experimentally demonstrated as long ago as 1897 by Binet in the course of his preliminary work on intelligence tests. Binet submitted a number of young persons to tests in which they were required to describe pictures and diagrams after viewing them for a given time.[2]

Another psychologist, Jaffa, devised an experiment in which two persons, by previous arrangement, simulated a violent quarrel in the presence of unsuspecting witnesses, who were then asked to make depositions in the belief that these would be used as evidence in court proceedings.[3]

This technique was elaborated by Varendonck, who arranged for a man to burst into his lecture-room, exchange a few heated words with him, and then leave abruptly. The students who had been in the room were subsequently questioned about the appearance and actions of the intruder, and asked to state after each reply whether they would be prepared to repeat it on oath. The interrupter was fair haired. Of the seventeen students who had observed him only one stated this correctly, while another scored a "near miss" with "light chestnut." Neither of them was sufficiently certain to state this as on oath. Of the fifteen who gave incorrect replies, however, seven were prepared to swear by their statements.

Other answers concerning the man's appearance and actions were equally inaccurate. Of a letter which he had attempted to give to Varendonck only three students remembered whether it was in an envelope, although fifteen recalled that it was white. The name of the sender of the letter had been clearly spoken, but nobody remembered it. Only two could say whether the man had actually approached Varendonck, and only one remembered the word he shouted as he departed. Of a total of 325 replies given only 116 were even approximately correct, while out of seventy-four statements which the students were prepared to swear on oath, less than half were anywhere near correct.[4]

An ingenious experiment was conducted along not dissimilar lines in 1960, by A. D. Cornell at a Cambridge cinema. By arrangement with the management of the cinema concerned, Cornell, draped in a white sheet, walked across the stage in front of the screen and then back again while a normal film was being shown. Members of the audience, who had not known that the experiment was to take place, were afterwards asked for their observations. Thirty-two per cent said they had seen *nothing* except what was on the screen, and among those who claimed to have seen *something* there was little agreement, as the following descriptions from different persons demonstrate:

A series of ellipses that turned into a friar.
A man walking backwards from left to right.
A young girl dressed in a white summer frock.
A woman dressed in a heavy coat with a scarf tied round her head.
A woman walking from left to right dressed in a sari.
A fault in the film that moved from right to left.
A person in a white dressing gown.
A woman's figure which was very small on the left but grew larger as it moved to the right.
A white polar bear ambling across the screen from left to right.

Only three undergraduates, one woman and her husband actually described the figure as dressed in a white sheet, and but one person, a woman, recognized the figure as "a man dressed up in a white sheet pretending to be a ghost." Her friend, who had been sitting next to her, saw nothing unusual at all. Even the projectionist, who had been watching the film through his observation window, saw absolutely nothing except the film.[5]

These results were obtained in reasonably good observational conditions. That an even lower degree of accuracy would result from the emotional atmosphere of the seance-room was ably demonstrated in the classic "imitation seance" experiments carried out in 1886, by S. J. Davey and Richard Hodgson.

Davey, who had become interested in spiritualism as the result of the death of a friend, became suspicious of some of the phenomena he witnessed at seances, and devised methods of reproducing such phenomena by normal means. He became outstandingly successful at this, so much so that many who had attended his "seances" became convinced he was a genuine medium. He excelled particularly at "slate-writing," a then fashionable form of mediumship, and was soon able to imitate all the phenomena produced by "genuine" slate-writing mediums.

Hodgson, realizing the opportunities such "imitation" seances provided for obtaining valuable information as to the reliability of witnesses, arranged with Davey for a series of sittings to be held at which all the "phenomena" were prearranged. He invited carefully chosen witnesses to take part, including several prominent members of the Society for Psychical Research. Immediately after each seance the sitters were asked to write down everything they could remember of what took place during the seance. Hodgson and Davey afterwards made an exhaustive analysis of these reports, showing how widely the accounts differed from the actual occurrences, and thereby demonstrating that evidence resting solely on the statements of eye-witnesses is by no means reliable. The following extracts from the accounts of witnesses at one of these sittings are typical.

A Mrs. Johnson stated that before the seance commenced the room was thoroughly searched and that the "medium" emptied his pockets. The door was then locked and sealed, the lights extinguished, and the sitters, including Davey, held hands around a table. Knocks were heard and bright lights seen, and a musical box which had been placed on the table floated, playing, into the air. The head of a woman appeared, followed by the figure of a man which, after bowing, disappeared through the ceiling. Mrs. Johnson could offer no explanation of the phenomena.

A Miss Wilson also described how the room had been searched and the door secured, and declared that a female head had materialized in good light, after which there appeared a bearded man, who was reading a book and who disappeared through the ceiling. She was certain that Davey's hands were held tightly throughout the seance by the sitters on either side of him, and that when the light was put on afterwards the door was still secured as before the seance commenced.

A third sitter, Mr. Rait, gave an even more dramatic account. He too described the securing of the door, but insisted that nothing was prepared in advance, the sitting being quite a casual one. He claimed to have heard raps and to have been touched by a cold, clammy hand; to have seen a light floating over the sitters which developed into an apparition "frightful in its ugliness," with distinct features resembling the head of a mummy. This was followed by another light which gradually took on the appearance of a bearded Oriental, with stony, fixed eyes and a vacant, listless expression. Like the others, he also certified that at the end of the seance the door was still properly locked and sealed.

In actual fact the sitting was quite different from any of these descriptions. Far from being a casual business, the procedure had been thoroughly worked out and rehearsed. Davey *did* lock the door at the beginning of the seance, but immediately unlocked it again. The articles used in the production of the "materializations" were hidden under a bookcase, and were not noticed when the room was searched because Davey created a diversion by turning out his pockets as the searchers approached. The phenomena were engineered by an assistant, a Mr. Munro, who entered by the unlocked door, any noise he made in so doing being drowned by the sound of the musical box. The first "materialization" was a mask covered with muslin (treated with luminous paint), and the second was Mr. Munro standing on the back of the "medium's" chair, his face visible in the reflected light from the pages (also coated with luminous paint) of an open book which he held before him. The noise as the first "spirit" vanished was accidental, but was accepted by the sitters as having been made when the phantom "disappeared through the ceiling." The raps were produced by Munro with a long stick which he had brought with him, and it was he who waved the musical box in the air. The "cold, clammy hand" was also Munro's. He had rolled up his sleeve and held his hand and forearm in a jug of water before entering the room.[6]

Although Davey and Hodgson afterwards made it quite clear that all the phenomena were produced by perfectly normal methods, a number of leading spiritualists absolutely refused to believe this, challenging Davey to reveal his methods. This he could not do without rendering future tests, which he hoped to make, impracticable, but in 1890, Davey died and in 1891, Alfred Russel Wallace renewed the challenge to Hodgson in a letter published in the *Journal* of the Society for Psychical Research.

"If such experiments . . . are clearly and fully explained as mechanical or sleight-of-hand tricks, available under the conditions usually adopted by professional mediums, it will do more to weaken the evidence for spiritualistic phenomena than anything that has yet been adduced by disbelievers. As one of the witnesses says, 'I believe that a full explanation of his methods would "fire a shot heard round the world" in almost every civilized community where the phenomena of so-called "spiritualism" are perplexing, and often madden true and good people.' But to have this effect it will not do to explain *some* of the phenomena by trick, leaving the more mysterious unsolved. They are claimed to be *all* trick, and unless *all* can be so explained many of us will be confirmed in our belief that Mr. Davey was really a medium as well as a conjuror, and that imputing all his performances to 'trick' he was deceiving the Society and the public."[7]

Wallace's challenge was taken up by Hodgson, who demonstrated quite conclusively that all Davey's phenomena were produced in a perfectly normal manner, giving a detailed description of the methods by which the "tricks" were carried out. The subject was also discussed at a meeting of the Society for Psychical Research on May 27, 1892, when Munro, Davey's former assistant, gave further information concerning his part in the sittings. Another witness who had been present at several of them, Pearsall Smith, made a telling comment on "the illogical position taken up by those who will admit conjuring as an explanation when they know the trick, but when they themselves cannot explain how the phenomenon was produced assume that it cannot be explained by conjuring."

At the same meeting, F. W. H. Myers stated that although he believed such phenomena as Davey produced by conjuring did sometimes occur through agencies as yet unknown, he considered that "this was a reason for gratitude to Mr. Davey, who had placed the conditions of inquiry on a securer basis, by demonstrating, more convincingly perhaps than anyone before him, how limited was the power of attention and observation which the ordinary man could bring to bear upon even the apparently simplest phenomena. The proved existence of such limitations might impose caution in dealing with persons who had obvious temptations to deceive, but it in no way lessened the importance of the inquiry itself." Sir William (then Professor) Barrett "heartily concurred in what Mr. Myers had said."[8]

The contrast between the attitudes of Myers and Wallace is noteworthy. Although Myers possessed a strong, almost passionate belief in survival—he once said, "From my earliest childhood, from my very first recollections, the desire for eternal life has immeasurably eclipsed for me every other wish or hope"[9]—this did not, as in the case of Wallace, prevent him from maintaining a strictly objective attitude towards the subject. Compare, for instance, Wallace's eager acceptance of supernormal explanations with this cautious statement by Myers:

"And in the year 1848, certain events, whose precise nature is still in dispute, occurred in America, in consequence of which many persons were led to believe that under appropriate circumstances these sounds, these movements, these tangible apparitions, could be evoked or reproduced at will. On this basis the creed of 'Modern Spiritualism' has been upbuilt. And here arises the pressing question—notoriously still undecided, difficult and complex beyond any anticipation—as to whether supernormal phenomena of this *physical* kind do in fact occur at all; or whether they are in *all* cases—as they undoubtedly have been in *many* cases—the product of mere fraud or delusion. This question, as it seems to us, is one

Mrs. Henry Sidgwick. (Courtesy Society for Psychical Research, London.)

to which we are bound to give our most careful attention; and if we have as yet failed to attain a decisive view, it is not for want of laborious observation, continued by several of us throughout many years."[10]

Mrs. Henry Sidgwick, a woman of penetrating intellect, writing on "spirit" photography, makes the point in words no less telling for their moderation. "The question is how far an intelligent person ought to detect trickery of the kind here supposed—which is practically conjuring—how far he ought to expect to see all that goes on within his possible field of vision when someone else is trying to prevent his seeing it, and I believe that the majority of persons expect too much of themselves and others in this way. It is not a proof of stupidity to be unable to see when or how a trick is done; even conjurors cannot do this always, or they would not need to buy each other's tricks. The ordinary mistake of eye-witnesses who relate experiences of this kind is to over-estimate their powers of observation and memory. In particular the assertion 'I never for an instant lost sight of so and so,' if the 'never' extends over any considerable length of time, is generally, I think, untrue, and is almost certain to be untrue if the observer has attempted to guard simultaneously against all the ways in which he conceives that the trick may have been done. I believe that anyone who would endeavour conscientiously to write accounts of what he saw at a conjuring entertainment would convince himself of this; unless he convinced himself—as some spiritualists have done —that the conjuror is a medium. On this point I would refer to Mr. S. J. Davey's experiments, which appear to me to prove conclusively that intelligent persons thinking that they have the conditions under their own control may not only be taken in, but may believe the event to have occurred in such a way as to render the particular trick actually practised impossible."[11]

In fairness, it must be stressed that not all spiritualists share Wallace's regrettable lack of objectivity. The celebrated Stainton Moses was clear on the point, and once wrote, "Some people would recognize anything. A broom and a sheet are quite enough to make up a grandmother for some wild enthusiasts who go with the figure in their eye, and see what they wish to see . . . I have had pictures that might be anything in this or any other world sent to me, and gravely claimed as recognized portraits; palpable old women authenticated as 'my spirit brother dead seventeen years, as he would be if he had, etc.' "[12]

Moses was not always so objective, however, and he provides one of the striking examples of the "will to believe" ably summarized by E. J. Dingwall:

"There are many spiritualists who are unable to tell the difference between genuine and openly fraudulent mediumship.

Even when they are told that a certain experiment is performed by natural means they sometimes refuse to believe it. Sir [sic] A. R. Wallace thought Dr. Lynn's assistant was a medium (*Spiritualist,* Aug. 17th, 1877), and Stainton Moses declared that 'it is sheer nonsense to treat such performances as Maskelyne's, Lynn's, and some that have been shown at the Crystal Palace, as "common conjuring." ' Similarly, Mr. Joy doubted the trickery of Maskelyne and Cooke's imitation of the Davenports' performances (*Spiritualist,* May 15th, 1873), and in this he was supported by Messrs. Dixon and Coleman, such opinions being expressed as that 'so-called conjurors . . . are also very powerful mediums' and that Messrs. Maskelyne and Cooke are 'the best of living mediums' (*Ib.,* Dec. 18th, 1874, Oct. 8th, 15th, 1875). Even today there are certain spiritualists who believe that Mr. Harry Houdini is a powerful medium, because they cannot think how he makes his escape from boxes and tanks, an opinion which reminds one of that held by Mr. Damiani, who thought that Giordano's box escape was the result of mediumistic powers (*Medium and Daybreak,* April 2nd, 1886, p. 212)."[13]

It was such wild opinions as these, and in particular some exaggerated and highly inaccurate accounts of the fraudulent "slate-writing" mediums "Dr." Henry Slade and William Eglington, which prompted the Davey-Hodgson experiments. Although these experiments were frequently quoted and their lessons taken heed of by many later researchers, it is curious that no further work along these lines seems to have been done in the field of parapsychology until Theodore Besterman began his investigations in 1928.

In June, 1928, Besterman, then librarian and later investigation officer of the Society for Psychical Research, took advantage of the presence in England of a self-confessed fraudulent medium, Karl Kraus,* by arranging for him to give a demonstration in the SPR seance-room. Of the five sitters taking part, three were left under the impression that the seance was to be a genuine one.[14] Besterman realized, however, that although such seances, where

---

*It is noteworthy that the celebrated Continental psychical researcher, Baron von Schrenck-Notzing, persisted, despite Kraus's confession that *all* his phenomena were fraudulent, in believing that he was sometimes genuine.

sitters expected "the real thing," were in many respects an ideal method of investigating, it would not be possible thus to carry out the really large-scale experiments necessary to reach significant conclusions. In 1931, therefore, he devised a series of "imitation seances," in which the sitters were told in advance that the phenomena were to be produced by normal means and that they would be asked to describe afterwards what had occurred. Six seances were held, forty-two sitters each attending once. The procedure, which was carefully rehearsed, was repeated exactly at each sitting.

The "medium" sat at a small table facing the sitters. On the table were several articles including a trumpet, a tambourine, a bell, etc. A gramophone was repeatedly started and stopped, an interruption was staged, and, after due warning, a flashlight photograph was taken. After each sitting the sitters were asked to complete questionnaires. The questions were so arranged that a system of scoring was possible.

Analysis of the answers revealed that most sitters were hopelessly inaccurate in their observations, the scores ranging from 5.9 per cent to 61 per cent, and averaging only 33.9 per cent. Only one sitter achieved some measure of success with every question, and two sitters secured marks in their replies to only three out of fifteen questions. Only a quarter of the replies mentioned an interruption in which Besterman had gone out of the room, and less than a tenth the fact that he returned to his chair putting something (a white card) into his pocket. Estimates of the amount of time which elapsed from the commencement of the sitting until the flash varied from five to forty minutes, whereas the actual interval was carefully timed at nineteen minutes. Nobody noticed the movement of a luminous drumstick, although it was in a prominent position when the flash occurred. Scarcely any of the sitters were able to report correctly the positions of the objects as revealed by the flash.

Even more remarkable was the fact that many sitters experienced hallucinations and illusions, claiming to have witnessed phenomena which certainly did not occur. Many testified to having observed movements, particularly of the table, and others thought they had seen lights suspended in the air. Besterman's report concludes with the following summary:

1. There is a slight tendency to underrate the number of persons present at a sitting.

2. Sitters largely ignore disturbances that appear to be irrelevant to the sitting.

3. Sitters are to a considerable extent unable to report with which hand a movement has been performed.

4. The degree to which sitters correctly report the objects used in a sitting is primarily governed, apart from special circumstances, by the size of these objects.

5. Sitters are able only to a very limited extent to report under what conditions of visibility a phenomenon took place.

6. Sitters' reports of auditory conditions at the time of a phenomenon are untrustworthy and erratic.

7. There is a tendency greatly to underrate and greatly to exaggerate a short period of time.

8. Sitters are almost entirely unable to report correctly the scene revealed by a flash.

9. Of the illusions that occur the most extreme are those of movement.[15]

Similar results and confirmation of Besterman's conclusions were obtained in a repetition of his experiments organized by Mrs. K. M. Goldney and myself, in 1961, at the College of Psychic Science, London.[16]

The tendency to experience hallucinations and illusions is most strikingly illustrated in a report by Dr. E. J. Dingwall on a seance he once attended in Massachusetts, given by a famous physical medium, where some sitters claimed that "music as if by a full orchestra filled the seance room: full form phantoms stood between the curtains of the cabinet presenting chalices out of which the sitters drank: materialized but invisible dogs lay on the laps of favoured sitters and were fondled by them."

"But," says Dingwall, "there were no phenomena whatever. Whilst the sitters listened to the exquisite music, I heard nothing, not even the strains of a distant radio. No materialized dog settled on my hands as I sat waiting. No phantom stood in the cabinet to hold out a chalice to me."

In Dingwall's opinion, the medium was an honest woman, the phenomena being "built up around her by a process of suggestion on the grand scale." The evidence, he thinks, suggested that "there were scarcely any phenomena with her beyond those supplied by the imagination of the sitters."[17]

I had a similar experience with a so-called "transfiguration" medium, for whom the claim was made that while in a trance her facial features changed and assumed the likenesses of deceased persons. I attended three of her seances by invitation, the other sitters on each occasion being regular members of her "circle." The procedure at each sitting was the same. The medium sat in a curtained recess in a corner of the room and the sitters, numbering about six, formed a rough semi-circle in front of her. The curtains were drawn back sufficiently for her whole body to be visible in the light of a small red lamp, the only illumination in the room. With much sighing and deep breathing the medium went into her "trance," and after a period of silence her husband (who was always present) whispered, "Look, the face is changing—it's the Chinaman." Within a few moments all the sitters were agreed that the features of the medium had been transformed into those of a venerable old Chinaman. He always appeared first, I was told, and his name, needless to say, was "Chang." Soon the husband announced and the sitters agreed that the face was fading, to be replaced in similar fashion by others apparently known and recognized by the sitters. The highlight of each sitting was the "appearance" of no less a spirit than that of George Bernard Shaw, who, it was claimed, never failed to honor this circle with his presence. The sitters, all seemingly serious, responsible people, were dismayed afterwards when, asked what I had seen, I could only reply, "Just the face of the medium."

The conclusions to be drawn from the foregoing are, to a large extent, self-evident, but they are important in influencing our approach to evidence and to its evaluation.

It seems irrefutable that the average witness is highly unreliable even in comparatively straightforward cases of observing and reporting, as the experiments of Binet, Varendonck, Besterman and Cornell demonstrate. When the witness has strong preconceived ideas, even greater inaccuracy may be expected; for example, it is not unknown for a scientist to see, in the results of an experiment, that which his theories led him to expect, although the work of others subsequently proved that it could not have been so. Similarly, where a strong emotional factor is present, as at seances, demonstrations, or other spiritualist activities, the tendency to mal-observation, self-deception, hallucination, self-persuasion after the event, and illusion is similarly enhanced—as illustrated by the reports of Besterman and Dingwall, quoted above.

It also seems irrefutable that a witness's intelligence and integrity provide no guarantee of his accuracy, any more than his belief in his own testimony does; these points are illustrated by the controversy over Davey's "mock" seances. Indeed, if a witness holds a passionate conviction of the truth of his evidence, this can indicate an emotional bias, a "will to believe," which may actually reduce the reliability of his testimony.

From consideration of these factors, we can deduce some of the principles to apply in collecting and evaluating evidence of allegedly paranormal happenings.

For one thing, a full written record should be made as soon as possible after the event, to minimize the chances of memory becoming blurred and distorted with the lapse of time. Further, a similar separate account should be obtained not merely from the central characters but from everyone connected with the event, however remotely. In compiling such accounts, witnesses may be prompted by questions from an experienced investigator, but these questions should be carefully framed not to suggest any particular answer—a suggestible witness may be unconsciously influenced to give the answer that he feels is expected, or to exaggerate the features of his story that seem to give rise to most interest.

These written records have the merit of minimizing the effect that one witness's story can have on another's; if the witnesses continue merely to give verbal accounts of their experience it is surprising how, after frequent re-tellings, one account can become contaminated by the other, until neither witness is certain what he actually experienced himself and what he "knows" must have happened. An early written account also has the merit of putting all aspects of the happening indisputably on record, so that if a particular feature is found to be more significant than was at first realized, there is no danger of witnesses unconsciously "twisting" their later version of it to enhance its value. To avoid possible dispute in such circumstances, all accounts should be signed and dated in the presence of a witness, and any later additions should be clearly shown as such.

The evidence of each witness should be checked against the other accounts, and any discrepancies noted; even if these do not relate directly to the allegedly paranormal happening, they may indicate the degree of reliance that can be placed on the witness's accuracy, or may suggest useful supplementary questions to be raised. Similarly, all statements of fact should be checked in every way possible—dates, times, addresses, weather, geography, topography, etc.—for these, too, may illustrate or may contradict an apparently inexplicable story.

These standards may sound unduly harsh and exacting, but it will be evident why they are the standards a good and reliable investigator aims at. He will, in fact, follow the method laid down by the legal authority whom I quoted earlier in this chapter, "to cross-examine [the witness] as to the sources of his knowledge; his reasons for believing the fact to be as he has stated; his reasons for recollecting it; the circumstances attending its occurrence; whether it was light or dark; and whether he was near or distant at the time it occurred, and the like; so that the jury may be able to judge of the degree of confidence they should place in the witness's testimony." The need in parapsychology for such detailed analysis is indicated by the same legal authority, who writes that less scrupulous enquiry may be called for when a fact seems probable than when it does not, for if a witness "tells of a fact having occurred which is contrary to common experience and observation, it will require that his integrity, veracity, and means of knowledge should be indisputable to induce anyone to believe it . . . The strength of the evidence should always be great in proportion to the improbability of the fact to be established by it." The investigator of the paranormal must accordingly aim at complete factual accuracy, not only for the sake of convincing sceptics but for his own satisfaction.

REFERENCES

1. Archbold: *Pleading, Evidence & Practice in Criminal Cases.* 35th edition, London, 1962.
2. Binet, A.: Psychologie individuelle — la description d'un objet, *L'Année Psychologique,* 1897. (Quoted by Besterman (15) below.)
3. Jaffa, S.: Ein psychologisches Experiment im Kriminal-seminar der Universität Berlin, *Beiträge zur Psychologie der Aussage,* 1913. (Quoted by Besterman (15) below.)
4. Varendonck, J.: *Experimenteele Bijdrage tot de Psychologie van het Getuigenis.* 1921. (An account in English of Varendonck's experiment is given by C. E. Bechhofer Roberts in *The Truth About Spiritualism.* London, 1932, pp. 80-82.)
5. Cornell, A. D.: Further experiments in apparitional observation, *Journ. SPR, XL*: 706:409-418.
6. Hodgson, R., and Davey, S. J.: The possibilities of malobservation and lapse of memory, *Proc. SPR, IV*:381-495, and *VIII*:253-310.
7. Wallace, A. R.: *Journ. SPR, V*: 78:43.
8. Society for Psychical Research, Report of a General Meeting, *Journ. SPR, V*:267-8.
9. Myers, F. W. H.: *Human Personality and its Survival of Bodily Death.* Vol. II, London, 1903.
10. Gurney, Edmund, Myers, F. W. H., and Podmore, Frank: *Phantasms of the Living.* London, 1886.
11. Sidgwick, Mrs. H.: On spirit photography, *Proc. SPR, VII*:276.
12. Moses, Wm. Stainton: *Human Nature.* May, 1875, p. 202.
13. Dingwall, E. J.: Magic and Mediumship, *Psychic Research Quarterly, I*: 3:216.
14. Besterman, T.: Report of a pseudo-sitting for psychical phenomena with Karl Kraus, *Journ. SPR, XXIV*: 450:38.
15. Besterman, T.: The psychology of testimony in relation to paraphysical phenomena, *Proc. SPR, XL*:367-87.
16. Edmunds, Simeon: Report of an experiment, *Light, LXXXI*: 3447:16-19.
17. Dingwall, E. J.: *Some Human Oddities.* London, 1947.

Chapter 11

TESTIMONY AND HUMAN FALLIBILITY

> *"Where the miraculous is concerned, neither considerable*
> *intellectual ability, nor undoubted honesty, nor knowledge*
> *of the world, nor proved faithfulness as civil historians,*
> *nor profound piety, on the part of eye-witnesses and*
> *contemporaries, affords any guarantee of the objective*
> *truth of their statements, when we know that a firm*
> *belief in the miraculous was ingrained in their minds,*
> *and was the pre-supposition of their*
> *observations and reasonings."*
>
> T. H. HUXLEY

In the last chapter, I mentioned the "will to believe" and the readiness of some people, including the more credulous spiritualists, to ascribe supernormal explanations to perfectly normal events. Many of the best-known accounts of "psychic" experiences owe both their origin and their wide acceptance to these factors; in other instances completely groundless stories have come to be regarded as fact simply because people *wanted* to believe them, and many charlatans have found willing victims for the same reasons. In this chapter, I shall outline examples from each of these categories, describing first the occurrences as claimed and then the findings of psychical researchers concerning them. In this way, I hope to show not only how stories originated and frauds were perpetrated but also the methods by which they were investigated. Let us start with one of the best known and most widely accepted of all "ghost stories," the famous Versailles "adventure."

On August 10, 1901, two English ladies, while staying in Paris, paid a visit to Versailles. Both scholars of high academic standing, one, Miss C. A. E. Moberly, was Principal of St. Hugh's College, Oxford, and the other, Miss E. F. Jourdain, was subsequently to succeed her. Ten years afterwards they published pseudonymously an account of their visit in a book, which was to become famous, entitled *An Adventure*. In a later edition, published in 1924, the authors revealed their identities. Their story, briefly, is this:

After spending some hours sightseeing, these two ladies decided to look for the Petit Trianon, formerly the retreat of Marie Antoinette. They lost their way, and then began to experience strange feelings, described by one as "an extraordinary depression," and by the other as "a dreamy unnatural oppression." The scenery, too, seemed to take on a strange appearance, "like a wood worked in tapestry." As they reached the junction of two paths, they saw two men wearing peculiar green uniforms, of whom they asked the way. "Afterwards we spoke of them as gardeners, because we remembered a wheelbarrow of some kind close by and the look of a pointed spade, but they were really very dignified officials, dressed in long greyish-green coats with small three-cornered hats."

Next, they came to a small circular kiosk near which sat a man wearing a cloak and a large shady hat. "The man's face was most repulsive—its expression odious." At that moment they heard the sound of someone running. No one else had been in sight, but another man suddenly appeared, "who had, apparently, just come either over or through the rock (or whatever it was) that shut out the view at the junction of the paths." This man, who also wore a cloak and a large sombrero hat, was greatly excited, and had a "most peculiar smile." He seemed to be insisting that they take a path to the right, which led over a small rustic bridge through a wood and thus to the Petit Trianon. As they approached it, they passed a strangely dressed woman sitting on a seat. On reaching the house, they saw a door open suddenly and a young man, "with the jaunty manner of a footman" appear. He looked "inquisitively amused" as he walked beside them and gave directions. After joining a party of sightseers and being shown over the house by a guide, the two ladies returned to Paris.

They did not discuss the events of that afternoon until a week later, when Miss Moberly asked her companion whether she thought the Petit Trianon was haunted. Miss Jourdain replied promptly, "Yes, I do," and added that she first formed this impression when they were walking in the gardens at Versailles. They did not speak of the matter again until three months later, when comparing notes, they decided they had "a new element of mystery" and agreed "to write down independent accounts of our expedition to Trianon, read up its history, and make every enquiry about the place."

As the result of their researches, which included extensive reading, the examination of original documents, hunting through archives and several subsequent visits to Versailles, these ladies concluded that they had taken some strange step backwards in time, had seen things as they were during the French Revolution of 1789, and had "entered within an act of the Queen's memory when alive" —the queen, of course, being Marie Antoinette. The two "gardeners," they decided, were brothers named Bersy, who, according to the records, were likely to have been on guard when the Queen was in residence at the Trianon. The man with the repulsive face was thought to be the Comte de Vaudreuil, an intimate friend of Marie Antoinette, while the running man with the peculiar smile was accepted as a messenger sent to warn the Queen of the approach of the mob from Paris. The woman sitting near the Trianon was the Queen herself; this, they maintained, was established by the resemblance to a portrait by Wertmüller, and by contemporary descriptions of the clothes worn by her. The man with the manner of a footman fitted in as one Lagrange, who, in 1789, was porter in charge of the *porte du perron de la chapelle*.

It was claimed that buildings, implements and other objects they had seen during their walk, but which did not in fact exist in 1901, were shown by early maps and records to have existed in 1789. These included the kiosk and the bridge, a waterfall, a grotto and an old-fashioned plough. The door from which their guide had emerged was from an old chapel which had fallen into disuse many years before their visit. The topography, too, was that of Versailles at the time of the Revolution.

Such material, suitably embellished and colorfully set out, forms the basis of *An Adventure*. The second half of the book is devoted to "results of research," an account of the subsequent discovery of facts thought to support the authors' explanation of their experience.

The immediate success of *An Adventure* and the interest it

evoked were phenomenal. The first edition was reprinted seven times, a second edition appeared in 1913, and others followed in 1924, 1931 and 1955. It has been, and still is, widely accepted as one of the best authenticated ghost stories of all time. As Lucille Iremonger puts it: "For fifty odd years it has commanded the respectful attention not only of the tellers of tales by the ingle-nook but of philosophers, scientists, scholars and sceptics of standing, and wherever it has been mentioned, whether in pub or in common room, at dinner table or on brains trust, passionate controversy has always ensued." On the reasons for this the same authority comments:

"The story went forth into the world as the work of two ladies whose truthfulness, although they adopted pseudonyms, was guaranteed by one of the most reputable of English publishers. When their disguise was finally abandoned they were known to the general public, as they had long been known among their acquaintances, to have been at the time of the adventure the Principal and the Vice-Principal-elect of an Oxford women's college.

"Never had such a story come from such a source. The style in which *An Adventure* was written—scholarly, restrained, scrupulously precise and unemotional—confirmed what one might have expected from women of such standing. It was clear, surely, that here were women beyond suspicion, of unimpeachable veracity, of the loftiest standards, of the highest integrity—and, moreover, of unquestioned intellectual powers."[1]

Spiritualists, of course, hailed the story enthusiastically as confirming their beliefs, and the spiritualist press, loyally if unskillfully, has constantly defended it against all attacks. And to be fair it must be said that many such attacks have been unfair and ill-informed. With these we need not concern ourselves, however, for, alas for Miss Moberly and Miss Jourdain, there are many good grounds upon which serious criticisms have been based. Let us now look at the other side of the coin.

Except for a "descriptive letter," which Miss Moberly claimed to have written within a week of the "adventure" but which was never quoted or produced, the first accounts were written some three months after the alleged experiences. During the intervening period, Miss Jourdain wrote to Miss Moberly saying she had been told of a tradition that Marie Antoinette and various members of her Court haunted Versailles. Thus, in addition to the tricks of memory which would be bound to color such a complex story after such a long period, there is good reason for assuming that a certain amount of mutual suggestion also occurred.

The first edition of *An Adventure* contained what purported to be two *independent* accounts, each written by one of the authors without consulting the other, and it is in the belief that this is so that the story is usually regarded. These accounts, usually designated M2 and J2, are known, however, to have been written some time, probably several years, after the original accounts (M1 and J1) were written at the end of 1901. When M2 and J2 were written the authors had, of course, read each other's first accounts and discussed them. (M1 and J1 appear as appendices in the second edition, but were omitted from subsequent ones. Copies of the second edition are rarely seen and almost impossible to obtain.) Clearly then, it is misleading to refer to M2 and J2 as *independent* accounts. This would be of less moment were the two accounts substantially the same; but in fact they differ widely—and significantly. These differences were summarized by W. H. Salter in a valuable "note" in the *Journal* of the SPR in 1950. I quote:

"It is mainly on the authority of M2 and J2 that the case has usually been judged, and it is accordingly important to know the date and history of these accounts. M1 and J1 were, according to a statement made by Miss Moberly in April 1911 to Miss Alice Johnson, then Research Officer of the SPR, 'written to each other, who knew every detail of the scenery,' or as stated in the second edition, 'for the purpose of finding out whom we had seen in common.' M2 and J2 were, according to the second edition, 'of a more descriptive character and were written for those who had not seen the place . . . It was not until 1904, on discovering the changed aspect of the grounds, that we attached any importance to B1, two papers [i.e., M2 and J2]. They were copied (with introductory sentences) into an MS book in 1906, and then destroyed.'

"The first point to note here is that, as M1 was written for Miss Jourdain, and J1 for Miss Moberly, it must be presumed that each read the other's first account before compiling her own second account. This presumption is, as we shall see, supported by the internal evidence, there being various points in which M2 and J2 resemble each other while differing from M1 and J1 respectively. In the advertisement of the first edition it is said that 'the book contains independent accounts by the two authors,' a statement hard to reconcile with the facts.

"The reason for compiling M2 and J2 is stated to have been to write a more descriptive account 'for those who had not seen the place,' and this was doubtless the authors' intention. But they went far beyond it, as may be seen by comparing the descriptions of the persons seen, the second accounts varying considerably from the first. Thus, the two men 'who appeared to be gardeners' of M1 become 'really very dignified officials' in M2. J1 mentions a woman and a girl seen together without describing their dress: in J2, it is said, 'I particularly noticed their unusual dress,' and this takes about thirty words to describe. Next, there is the man seated by the Temple de l'Amour (or Pavillon de Musique or whatever it was); M1 described his face as 'most repulsive': M2 says 'his complexion was very dark and rough'; J1 says 'his expression was very evil,' J2 adds that his face 'was marked by smallpox: his complexion was very dark.' Immediately after this is the incident of the running man, described in M1 as 'apparently coming over the rock (or whatever it was)': in M2, it is said that he 'had apparently just come either over or through the rock (or whatever it was).' In M1, Miss Moberly 'could not follow the words he said'; in M2, she gives him fourteen words with comments on his accent, on which J1 had already remarked.

"Up to this point the two authors had seen the same six persons, though not in the same order. But near the Petit Trianon building Miss Moberly saw a woman sketching, whom Miss Jourdain did not remember seeing. M1 describes this lady and her dress; M2 gives a rather fuller description, and adds that she thought 'her dress was rather old-fashioned and unusual.' Last there is the young man (M1) or boy (J1) who came out of the Petit Trianon. M2 adds that he came out 'banging the door behind him'; J2 also adds the slamming of a door. The significance of this is that he appeared to come from the direction of a door that was bangable in the eighteenth century, but had been permanently closed for some years in 1901.

"It will be seen that as regards all the eight persons mentioned by Miss Moberly, and the seven mentioned by Miss Jourdain, alterations are made in M2 or J2 or both, as regards the descriptions of their appearance or behaviour, and that the alterations are in each case such as to make it more difficult to fit the persons into the actual scene of 1901."[2]

That the memories of the authors were far from reliable is clearly shown by their vagueness concerning the dates at which M2 and J2 were written. In the second edition of *An Adventure,* it was claimed that these were within a month or so of M1 and J1. In 1902, however, they attempted to interest the SPR in their story and sent M1 and J1 for examination. Here Salter comments: "These documents were examined by Mrs. Sidgwick . . . She did not think there was enough in M1 and J1 to serve as a basis for an investigation. Had the much fuller accounts given in M2 and J2 then been in existence, it is reasonable to suppose that they would have been shown to Mrs. Sidgwick, together perhaps with M1 and J1 and an explanation of the relation between the two sets of documents."

In 1911, the authors explained to Miss Alice Johnson, then Research Officer of the SPR, that it was not until 1904 that certain topographical discoveries concerning Versailles, as it was in the eighteenth century, caused them to attach any importance to M2 and J2. Yet, for some obscure reason, in 1906 they copied these later accounts into a notebook and then destroyed the originals. Salter shows remarkable restraint when he observes: "It is not very easy to follow the authors' reasoning as stated in the second edition. Documents to which they say they did not attach 'any special importance' were preserved from November-December, 1901, until 1904, when they discovered 'the changed aspect of the grounds.' In 1904, they began their researches in the French National Archives, the result of which seems to have made their narratives all the more important, and then in 1906 they copy them into an MS book and destroy them. It is such an odd sequence of events as to suggest that the authors' memory of the dates of composition of M2 and J2 had in the interval between 1906 and 1911, become very hazy. Whether this is so or not, the destruction of original documents later to be published as the foundation of an extraordinary, supernormal experience reflects oddly on their standards of evidence."

An Adventure has many other weaknesses. For instance, no attempt was made to ascertain what persons, besides the authors, were actually in the gardens of the Petit Trianon on the day concerned. Nor was any real check made on the type of clothing one might have expected to see at Versailles in 1901. Here again Salter's comment is to the point:

"Were the authors right in supposing that the dress of the persons seen was not that of 1901? I shall not hazard an opinion as to whether the dress of the lady seen sketching might or might not have been worn by a woman artist in 1901, or whether it would have been 'unusual' for a girl of thirteen or fourteen, the daughter, it would seem, of a local employee, to have worn a dress reaching to her ankles in the Versailles gardens of that period, as described in J2. 'Unusual' it would have been in the England of 1901, but not at that time in several country districts on the Continent. As to the men, the uniform worn by the 'gardeners' does not seem to have been that of any persons employed in the gardens in 1901, but is it quite certain that it was not the uniform of other minor functionaries on a visit? France is full of all sorts of uniforms, and Versailles attracts visitors from all over the country. The cloaks and sombreros (or slouch hats) of the sitting and running men were, unless my recollection of that period is wholly wrong, an attire much affected by contemporary artists.

"Nothing is said by either of the authors in either of their accounts as to what any one of the five male persons, four men and a lad, wore on their legs. This is a matter in which the difference between 1792 and 1901 would leap to the eye of an observant person. Roughly speaking the difference is between breeches, the general wear of all ranks in 1792, and trousers, the universal wear in 1901, except for special occasions, such as Court Dress or sport. The silence of the authors on this crucial matter suggests that they observed no masculine leg-wear inappropriate to 1901, because there was none to observe. If that is so, then there is a strong presumption that all the male *dramatis personae* of 1901 were persons of the twentieth century, and inferentially that the females were so too.

"M. Sage, an Honorary Associate of the SPR, who was a Frenchman and knew Versailles well, gave it as his opinion in 1911 that all the supposed eighteenth-century persons described in the book might well have been met in the flesh in the Versailles of 1901.

"I have no desire to attempt to prove that Miss Moberly and Miss Jourdain had no remarkable experience on 10 August 1901. They thought at the time that they had had one, and when intelligent people in good health think that, they probably have. There are, however, many different kinds and gradations of experiences, from vague to precise, from purely subjective to veridical. But the authors recorded, investigated, and published their experience in such a way as to leave the whole affair in an impenetrable fog of uncertainty. All this would have been avoided if they had added to their many virtues some knowledge of the standards of evidence, and the recognized procedure for conforming to them, that the peculiar subject-matter of psychical research makes necessary. Contemporary records properly dated, independent attestation, careful inquiry, before any other research was begun, as to whether a normal explanation was possible—these were indispensable preliminaries for an investigation which, in view of the nature of the experience and the conditions in which it occurred, was in any event bound to be difficult. Through their failure to take these steps, their elaborate researches, conducted with an ability and perseverance worthy of all praise, rested on an insecure foundation. Their knowledge of French literature should have reminded them of the comment made by a French lady when told of an earlier and hardly less notable paranormal experience reported from the neighborhood of Paris, 'C'est le premier pas qui coute.' "*

For a really comprehensive study, not only of *An Adventure* itself, but also of the characters and environment of the authors

---

*The Marquise du Deffand in 1763, commenting on the legend that St. Denis walked two leagues carrying his head in his hands.

and of the other factors that make up the background of the story, Lucille Iremonger's book, *The Ghosts of Versailles*, cannot be too highly recommended. The honesty and sincerity of Miss Moberly and Miss Jourdain has never been seriously questioned. Their book is a record, to quote Salter again, "of how two extremely able women, starting out with the best intentions, muddled their case at an early stage so completely as to make all their later labors useless: and all because they had not joined the SPR!"

The SPR has not always been blameless, however. One of the best (or worst, whichever way you look at it) examples of the danger of accepting an uncorroborated story lies at the door of two of its most respected officers. The case is well-known, but its importance warrants inclusion here.

In 1884, the SPR received a report from Sir Edmund Hornby, Chief Judge of the Supreme Consular Court of China and Japan. One evening in 1874, as was his custom, he had written out his judgements for the day and left them with his butler to be given to a newspaper reporter who used to call regularly to collect these reports. During the night he was awakened by a tap at his door and was astonished to see the reporter, looking deathly pale, standing in the doorway. Thinking the man had mistakenly come to the wrong room Sir Edmund directed him to that of the butler. Instead of leaving, however, he came to the foot of the bed and politely but insistently pleaded to be given a verbal summary of the day's judgements. Strange though the request seemed, Sir Edmund, in order to avoid a disturbance, eventually did so; the reporter took shorthand notes, thanked the judge, and departed. Sir Edmund noted the time as half past one. He then described what had happened to Lady Hornby, who had been awakened by his conversation with the reporter. Next morning Sir Edmund learned that the man had died at his home during the night. His wife had seen him at a quarter to one and at half past one had found him dead. Beside him was his notebook, in which the last entry was a heading for a judgement. The reporter, who had died of heart disease, had not left his home that night, and the butler affirmed that no one could have got into Sir Edmund's house.

Relying presumably on the standing of their informant, the

SPR accepted the story and published it in its *Proceedings.*[3] It was also the subject of an article by F. W. H. Myers and Edmund Gurney in the *Nineteenth Century* of July, 1884. This article was seen by a Mr. F. H. Balfour, of Shanghai, who made some on-the-spot inquiries which he reported in a letter published in the same journal in November, 1884. His information was devastating. The reporter mentioned by Sir Edmund Hornby was in fact Mr. Hugh Lang, editor of the *Shanghai Courier,* who had died between 8:00 a.m. and 9:00 a.m. on January 21, 1875. No judgements were made on the preceding day. Further, Sir Edmund did not marry until three months after Lang's death. When these facts were put to him, Sir Edmund apologized and agreed that his memory had played him false.

Here, as with *An Adventure,* it has not been seriously suggested that the story was a deliberate fabrication. Sir Edmund may well have had a vivid dream of the dead reporter, whom he knew well, and have come, by various tricks of memory, to believe sincerely in the truth of the account he gave to the SPR. Be that as it may, he still did a valuable service to psychical research, though unwittingly, by demonstrating that even a trained legal mind can be self-deceived, and by driving home the danger of accepting uncorroborated evidence, however authoritative its source.

It seems clear that both Sir Edmund Hornby's story and *An Adventure* originated in good faith and were entertained because they were seemingly on good authority. The origins of some other stories that have gained wide credence are much more doubtful. This is particularly true of many of the more colorful claims for the powers of spiritualist mediums, especially when the medium concerned is a professional and stands to gain in reputation by the acceptance of such stories. A classic example of the way in which an unsupported claim can gain widespread acceptance purely through constant repetition and the repeated assertion that it is true is the popular belief that the identity of "Jack the Ripper," the notorious nineteenth century mass murderer, was made known to the police by a clairvoyant. The story, briefly, is as follows:

Early on the morning of August 7, 1888, the body of a middle-aged woman, later identified as a prostitute who lived in the district, was found on the landing of a cheap Whitechapel lodging-house. On the body were no less than thirty deep knife wounds.

There were no clues to indicate the identity of the murderer, and there was no apparent motive for the crime. The victim was almost penniless, friendless, but, so far as could be ascertained, without enemies. What little public interest the murder aroused had barely subsided, however, when, on August 31, another woman of the same type was found murdered in similar circumstances in the same district.

She too had been stabbed, but in addition her body had been mutilated, and the manner in which this was carried out indicated that the murderer possessed a fair knowledge, at least, of human anatomy. As in the first case, the victim appeared to have had no enemies, and the killing seemed purposeless.

A week later a third woman, also a prostitute, was found dead and mutilated in Whitechapel, and this time an organ had been detached from the body. It was apparent that the operation could only have been performed by someone with the skill and anatomical knowledge of a surgeon or, less probably, an exceptionally competent slaughterman, and even so, would have taken at least fifteen minutes to carry out.

On October 1, within an hour, two more prostitutes were killed, again in the Whitechapel district. Only the body of the second of these was mutilated, presumably because the murderer was disturbed in his attempt with the first. The following morning a postcard, postmarked the previous night and signed "Jack the Ripper," was received by the Central News Agency. Part of it read, "You'll hear about Saucy Jack's work tomorrow. Double event this time. Number one squealed a bit, couldn't finish straight off." Some days later a parcel was received by Mr. George Lusk, a member of a group of "vigilants" which had been patrolling the streets of Whitechapel in an attempt to forestall further killings. It contained part of a human kidney and a note which read, "From Hell —Mr. Lusk. Sir—I send you half the kidne I took from one woman, prasarved it for you, tother piece I fried and ate; it was very nice. I may send you the bloody knif that took it out if you only wate a little longer. Catch me when you can, Mr. Lusk."

Nothing more was heard of "Jack" until November 9. On the morning of that day, a rent-collector called at a house in Miller Court, Whitechapel. He found the door of one room locked, looked in at the window, and almost fainted with horror, for the tenant had been killed, her body hacked to pieces and scattered about the room. In this instance there was no evidence of any surgical skill, the body having been disembowelled and crudely cut up. That the man who had committed this murder was insane was clear beyond all doubt.

This was the last of the murders attributed to Jack the Ripper. No more similar crimes were committed around that time in the Whitechapel area, and no further letters were received from him. No one was ever brought to trial for these crimes, which today remain as great a mystery as ever.

Many theories, of course, have been put forward, some plausible, many highly improbable. One suggestion was that the murderer was a butcher on a cattle-boat making regular trips to London, another that he was a doctor intent on avenging the infection of his son with venereal disease by a Whitechapel prostitute. There appears to be no factual backing for any of them.

Public fancy seems to have been captured most successfully, however, by the widely publicized and oft-repeated story that the true identity of the killer was revealed to the police by a famous spiritualist medium, Robert James Lees.

Lees, who was also well known as an author and journalist, is reputed to have rendered service as a medium to Queen Victoria, for which he was awarded a pension from the Privy Purse. The story of how he is supposed to have "tracked down" Jack the Ripper, first published in 1895 and subsequently repeated in a variety of periodicals, is, in essence, as follows.

During the period of Jack the Ripper's activities, Lees was at work in his study one day when he suddenly had a clairvoyant "vision" in which a gruesome scene was acted out. He seemed to see a man, wearing a dark suit made of Scotch tweed, walking with a woman along a mean-looking street. The couple turned into a narrow court, the name of which Lees saw quite clearly. He also noticed that the time, as shown on a clock in a nearby "gin palace," was 12:40 a.m. Suddenly the man covered the woman's mouth with one hand, drew a knife with the other and then cut her throat. The woman, who was half drunk, could only offer feeble resistance. After killing her the man gashed her body in various places.

Lees reported his experience to Scotland Yard, but it was ignored. The following night, however, a woman was murdered at the same time and place, and in exactly the same manner, as Lees had foreseen in his "vision."

Shortly before another "Ripper" murder, Lees received, in the same way, a forewarning that it would occur; he also foresaw that the victim's ears would be cut off. On this occasion, Scotland Yard took far more notice, for a card bearing the signature "Jack the Ripper," which contained the statement that the next victim would have her ears cut off, had just been received.

Lees had a similar experience in connection with the last of the "Ripper" murders, which he related to the police at Scotland Yard shortly before they were informed of the discovery of the body. As a consequence, the police asked him to try to use his strange faculty to track down the murderer. Lees consented, and accompanied an inspector to the scene of the crime. Then, like a bloodhound, he led the police on a trail which ended at the West End home of a well-known doctor, where he insisted that the murderer would be found. Somewhat sceptically, the police officers entered and questioned the doctor's wife, who eventually admitted that her husband was subject to fits of obsession during which he indulged in acts of fiendish cruelty. After an inquiry by a medical commission, he was sent to a private asylum for the insane at Islington. His name was never made public. In one version of the story, it is alleged that an announcement was made that the doctor had died of heart failure, and that a fake funeral took place in which an empty coffin was buried.

And there, for many years, the matter rested. The account, however often it was retold and rehashed, always made a good story. Dismissed, of course, by the sceptics, it was, nevertheless, accepted by many as factual, while the supporters of spiritualism not unnaturally acclaimed it as supporting their belief in the powers of mediums. Nothing, however, seems to have been done to check the authenticity of the story until 1948, when Dr. Donald J. West, then Research Officer of the Society for Psychical Research, began a systematic and thorough inquiry. Alas for the believers, his report was devastating.[4]

Dr. West dealt first with the origin and development of the story, which was originally published in the Chicago *Sunday Times and Herald* for April 28, 1895. Ostensibly it came from a friend who had heard the details from Lees himself. It was reproduced in the London *Daily Express* for March 9 and 10, 1931, and in *Le Matin* for March 21 and 22, 1931. More recent accounts appeared in *Cavalcade* in December, 1947, and *Fate* in May, 1949. It would be pointless, said West, to list all the periodicals and books in which the story has been quoted as evidence of spirit intervention.

After demonstrating that the accounts are unreliable in regard to detail and contain many serious distortions, Dr. West listed three "essential elements" of the story, namely:

1. The veridical impression about the ears being cut off.
2. The visits of Lees to Scotland Yard and their utilization of his powers by the police.
3. The identity and fate of the mad doctor.

He then considered each of these points individually.

Of (1) he first pointed out that the letter signed "Jack the Ripper" was received by the Central News Agency and not the police. It contained the statement, "The next job I do I shall clip the lady's ears off and send to the police officers just for jolly . . ." There was no justification for supposing that the author of this letter was really the murderer; it could have been a practical joker. In any event Lees was a journalist, and might well have learned of the existence of the letter from the news agency just as quickly as Scotland Yard.

To check the truth of point (2) Dr. West wrote a letter of inquiry to Scotland Yard. He received the following reply:

New Scotland Yard, S.W.1.
March 17, 1949

Sir,
    With reference to your letter of March 8, regarding the "Jack the Ripper" murders, I am directed by the Commissioner

to inform you that, according to the records in this office, there is no foundation for newspaper stories that the murderer was known to the Police, and traced through the aid of a medium.

I am to add that there is no record of the person named James Lees to whom you refer in your letter.

Signed

Secretary.

Dr. West also wrote to the Home Office, and received an equally emphatic denial. It read:

Home Office,

Whitehall,

December 29, 1948

Sir,

I am directed by the Secretary of State to refer to your letter of November 30 about the nineteenth-century murderer known as Jack the Ripper and to say that there is no reference in the records of the Department to the statement said to have been left by a medium named Lees and that no such file as you mention appears to exist.

Signed

C. S. Brown

Dr. West dealt with point (3) exhaustively. Here he took into account not only the various written versions of the story, but the statement made to him in a personal interview by the medium's daughter, Miss Eva Lees. She asserted that the identity of the murderer was known to her, but that she could not reveal it lest his descendants might suffer. She added that he was a well-known physician, a member of a titled family, and that his funeral had caused quite a stir.

Examination of the obituaries in *The Times* and the medical journals of the period, however, failed to substantiate these claims. No death of a prominent London physician is reported anywhere in the six months following the last "Jack the Ripper" murder.

Dr. West also made the telling comment that "if it were true that the identity of the Ripper was known to the police immediately after the commission of his last crime (November 9, 1888), this would be difficult to reconcile with the fact that subsequent arrests were made of persons believed to be involved in the murders."

The conclusion then must be that this story, like others beloved by many spiritualists and believers in "the occult," does not stand up to serious, impartial investigation. In the words of Dr. West, "the claim that the medium Lees helped to trace 'Jack the Ripper' is not supported by the known facts. Scotland Yard denies all knowledge of the medium, and no one can be found to fit the description of the mad doctor who was supposed to have disappeared."

Now let us turn to the discussion, promised in Chapter Five, of the case of Sir William Crookes and the medium Florence Cook, as it appears in the light of recent revelations.

During the early 1870s, considerable interest and controversy was aroused in spiritualistic circles by the claims made for a young medium at whose seances full-form materializations of spirit forms were said to appear and move freely among the sitters while she remained unconscious in the cabinet. One of these materializations was allegedly the spirit of a young woman named Katie King, daughter of the notorious pirate John King, alias Henry Morgan. Not everyone accepted these phenomena as genuine, however, and some openly accused her of fraud.

In 1874, Crookes, already famous in this field for his investigation of the physical medium D. D. Home, reported that he had made a thorough examination of Florence Cook's mediumship and found it genuine. He had not only witnessed full-form materializations, but had photographed them. He had, he declared, seen the entranced medium still in the "cabinet" at the same time as the materialized spirit of Katie King was walking about in the seance-room, and had carried on normal conversations with this spirit, and even, on one occasion, embraced her.

The testimony of such an eminent scientist raised Florence to a pinnacle of fame from which no amount of criticism has seemed able to dislodge her. It secured for her an important place in the history of spiritualism, and made her mediumship one of the cornerstones of the evidence for materialization phenomena. Leading parapsychologists who appear to have felt bound to accept Crookes's testimony include Charles Richet, Sir Oliver Lodge, René Sudre, P. T. Bret and George Zorab, while Crookes's biographer, E. E. Fournier d'Albe, a critical investigator himself, considered that all physical phenomena were ultimately based on Crookes's work and that the evidence for "authentic materializations" was confined to the Katie King affair.[5]

The importance to spiritualists of Crookes's report was illustrated in an article by one of spiritualism's leading British propagandists, B. Abdy Collins. The article, one of a series entitled "The Whole Case for Survival," contained these statements:

"The most important case of complete materialization of a human form, well known to spiritualists, is that of Katie King, who claimed to be Annie Owen de Morgan, daughter of the famous pirate Sir Henry Owen de Morgan, who became Governor of Jamaica."

After outlining the main points of Crookes's report and the statements of other witnesses Collins explained:

"I have devoted practically all my space to this one case because I feel that the materialization of complete figures which behave like ordinary persons in every way stands or falls by this one case . . .

"In view, however, of Sir William's position as a chemist of world wide renown, subsequently President of the Royal Society and of the British Association and other important societies, and winner of all the much prized medals of the Royal Society, and his continued asseveration of the accuracy of his results up till his death in 1919 forty-six years later, I do not see any ground whatever for distrusting any part of his testimony. And if it is accepted, then materialization must be a fact."[6]

Collins concluded his article by suggesting that materialization could explain the alleged resurrection of Christ, a view which has also been advanced by other spiritualists and by some prominent psychical researchers, notably George Zorab[7] and Lucian Landau.[8]

Prior to 1962, most of the controversy over Crookes's report turned on whether the phenomena were genuine or Crookes had been deceived by clever trickery on the part of the medium. In that year, however, valuable new light was thrown on the matter by the publication of the report of a painstaking investigation by an English researcher, Trevor H. Hall, entitled *The Spiritualists*. In the course of extensive enquiries, Hall unearthed much new material, which, he claims, shows conclusively that far from being deluded, Crookes was himself a leading partner in a gigantic hoax, the purpose of which was to cover up an illicit affair between the medium and himself. Whether or not one accepts the validity of Hall's conclusions, it must surely be agreed that he has performed a valuable service in drawing attention to this third alternative possibility, namely, that the phenomena produced by Florence Cook were fraudulent and that Crookes took part in producing them and added to the deception by issuing dishonest reports afterwards.

According to Hall, Florence Cook was launched on her dubious career, presumably for their own monetary gain, by Thomas Blyton, secretary to the Dalston Association of Inquirers into Spiritualism (which soon afterwards became the British National Association of Spiritualists), and W. H. Harrison, editor of a publication called *The Spiritualist*. Both the society and the publication were largely subsidized by a wealthy spiritualist named Charles Blackburn, to whom Florence was represented as a wonderful young medium and who, as a result, provided her with an income in order that she might devote all her time to developing her mediumship.

Harrison gave so much space in his paper to extravagant accounts of the young medium's prowess that the editor of a rival journal, *The Spiritual Magazine*, suggested that *The Spiritualist* should be re-named Miss Florence Cook's Journal. Both Harrison and Blyton clearly did all they could to give Florence a "build-up" for the benefit of their mutual backer.

Florence received training in mediumship from two well-known materialization mediums of the time, Frank Herne and Charles Williams, both of whom were later conclusively exposed as fraudulent. At one seance, when she and Herne were the mediums, a draped figure "came out into the passage shaking people by the hand, and leading or pushing them to one end of the passage leaving the end which led to the stairs clear . . . After a time, the spectators observed two shadows emerge from the dark room and ascend the stairs together. A few seconds later, the passage was plunged into pitch darkness and nothing was heard for a quarter of an hour, after which time the two alleged materializations presumably returned from their mysterious expedition upstairs."

Herne, it is noted, had also received financial assistance from the benevolent Mr. Blackburn.

At this time, there was considerable comment, by a variety of sitters, on the suspicious similarity of appearance in the faces of the medium and the materialized spirit, and accusations of downright fraud were soon to follow. In the issue of *The Lancet* dated January 10, 1874, it was reported:

"Mr. William Hipp has also recounted in the *Echo* his experience of a seance, with the celebrated Miss Cook as a medium. Among other manifestations the time arrived for the spirits to sprinkle the guests with water, a tumbler having been placed on the table for that purpose. The room was darkened and expectation was on tiptoe, but the sceptical Mr. Hipp grasped the tumbler, and in a few seconds clutched the hand that was dipped into it. As he had caught a spirit a light was procured, and a striking tableau presented itself. The spirit hand had an arm of flesh, which formed part of Miss Cook's body. The censure and ignominy, he adds, that he brought on himself was only counterbalanced by the satisfaction he felt in having at last caught a spirit."

A similar incident occurred within a few weeks of the exposure by Hipp. Mr. William Volckman, a spiritualist and, incidentally, a member of the Dialectical Society committee mentioned in Chapter One, had been trying for some months to obtain an invitation to one of Florence's seances, and was at last successful after acting on a hint from her father that a present of jewelry would not be refused by the medium. Here is Hall's account of what took place:

"During the sitting of December 9th, Katie King took Volckman by the hand, a gesture to all the sitters which had become habitual with her. His suspicions having been aroused by what he had observed during the sitting, he retained in his grasp first the hand and then the waist of the apparition, with the stated conviction that he was holding Florence Cook. The gas light was hastily extinguished and Edward Elgie Corner, who was to marry Florence

four months later, came to the rescue of 'Katie King,' assisted by
Mr. G. R. Tapp. After an undignified struggle the spirit was res-
cued from Volckman's grasp and retired hastily to the cabinet, the
scuffle being sufficiently unrestrained for Volckman to suffer the
loss of part of his beard and to receive other superficial injuries.
After an interval of five minutes the cabinet was opened and Florence was found in a distressed condition, but with the tape tied
round her waist as it had been at the beginning of the seance.
Volckman was escorted from the house, and the dishevelled medium was taken under the care of the lady sitters."

Unfortunately for Florence, Charles Blackburn was present at
the Volckman seance, and it appears that even his credulity was
stretched to the limit by what he had witnessed. Florence, faced
with the possible loss of her income, sought for a way of re-establish-
ing her reputation, and in desperation went to Crookes, whom she
had already met once and knew to be a keen psychical investigator.

The consequence of her visit to Crookes, and the details of his
subsequent "investigation" of Florence form the subject of Chap-
ters Two and Three of *The Spiritualists*. The author then proceeds, by way of a number of quotations from leading authorities
of the time who had expressed doubts concerning Crookes's investigations, to a consideration of the character of Crookes, drawing
corroboration in support of his conclusions from some independent
statements which have only recently been made public. Later chap-
ters deal with the later mediumship of Florence and that of her
sister Kate, who, after her sister's death in 1904, in turn married
Edward Corner; also the shocking but undoubtedly true story of
how the Cook family extorted huge sums of money from Charles
Blackburn in his feeble-minded old age by claiming that a spirit
had directed him to entrust his daughter, who had previously been
in an asylum, to their care.

Hall suggests that Florence Cook, by no means sexually innocent when she threw herself on the mercy of Crookes, exerted her
feminine wiles to such good effect that he became completely in-
fatuated with her. She stayed at his house during the time of his
investigations, and far from witnessing genuine phenomena, or
even being deceived by Florence, Crookes took a leading part in

the perpetration of a gigantic deception, the purposes of which were to cover up his own illicit association with her (Crookes was a married man with a large family), and to reinstate her in the eyes of her financial supporter, Charles Blackburn. Here are a few of the many facts set down by Trevor Hall in support of his thesis.

Instead of adhering to the critical scientific standards for which he was justly famed and respected, Crookes in this instance prejudged the issue in a most unscientific manner, referring in his preliminary report, made soon after the beginning of his "investigation," to "removing unjust suspicion which is cast upon another," and continuing, "And when this person is a woman—young, sensitive and innocent—it becomes especially a duty for me to give the weight of my testimony in favor of her whom I believe to be unjustly accused."

Crookes, for some reason which he never explained, chose to record the story of the miracles he claimed to have witnessed in a cheap and insignificant spiritualist paper rather than, as in the case of his previous work, in a learned scientific journal. His report contained the statement: "Miss Cook is now devoting herself exclusively to a series of private *seances* with *me and one or two friends*" (my italics). This is in strange contrast to Crookes's insistence, at the time of his experiments with D. D. Home, that scientific men of eminence should witness the phenomena in order to lend the weight of their testimony to the reports. There appears to be no corroboration of any of the phenomena Crookes claimed to have witnessed in his home, and the "one or two friends" seem to have consisted of Mrs. Helen Whittall, Florence Cook's sister Kate, and the infamous (as he later became through the notorious "Bravo Case") Dr. Gully. These names were not published by Crookes, and only became known after his death when they were found as signatures on the back of a photograph taken by Crookes which allegedly shows the materialized Katie King.

Cromwell Varley, the famous electrical engineer, who was also a spiritualist, devised an electrical apparatus for controlling the medium and this was employed, with interesting results, at one of the seances at Crookes's home. Nowhere, however, does Crookes make any mention of it.

When a number of contemporary researchers, in particular Serjeant Cox, criticized the conditions under which Crookes had reported that the seances were being held, their location was moved to the home of Florence Cook at Hackney before any of the critics were invited to attend. Cox, who had collaborated on most amicable terms with Crookes in the investigation of Home, repeatedly made a number of simple and reasonable suggestions as to methods of demonstrating clearly whether the medium was, as Crookes claimed, always in the cabinet when Katie King materialized, none of which Crookes would agree to employ.

Cox, who had attended a number of Florence Cook's seances previously, put his own opinion pungently in a letter to *The Spiritualist* dated April 23, 1874, pointing out that in his experience the materialization exactly resembled the medium "in face, hair, teeth, eyes, hands, and movements of the body." He suggested, not unreasonably, that proof could easily be established beyond all doubt by the simple process of drawing aside the curtain of the cabinet, but stated that this test had neither been proffered nor permitted at the seances he had attended. It is here noteworthy that *The Spiritualist* attempted to suppress Cox's letter and did not publish it until Cox had it printed in a rival paper, *The Medium and Daybreak*.

The location of the seances was moved, Hall believes, because the demands for a convincing demonstration that Florence and Katie King were separate beings had become insistent, and such a demonstration could only be effected by the introduction of an accomplice, a feat not practicable at Crookes's house but perfectly easy at that of Florence, where an arrangement of communicating doors existed. Confirmation of this view is contained in Dr. C. M. Davies's book *Mystic London,* in which he gives a first-hand account of one of the sittings. Part of it reads:

"We . . . moved up to the parlour floor, where two rooms communicated through folding doors, the front apartment being that in which we assembled, and the back used as a bedroom, where the ladies took off their 'things.' This latter room, be it remembered, had a second door communicating with the passage, and so with the universe of space in general. One leaf of the folding doors was closed, and a curtain hung over the other. Pillows were placed on the floor, just inside the curtain, and the little medium, who was nattily arrayed in a blue dress, was laid upon them. We were requested to sing and talk during the 'materialization,' and there was as much putting up and lowering of the light as in a modern sensation drama. The Professor [Crookes] acted all the time as Master of the Ceremonies, retaining his place at the aperture; and I fear, from the very first, exciting suspicion by his marked attentions, not to the medium, but to the ghost.''

Dr. Davies stated openly in his book that he suspected the presence of a confederate.

At one sitting, Charles Blackburn attended and was permitted to kiss Katie King. He found her cheek "soft and warm as velvet" and asked to see the medium in the cabinet, whereupon he was shown behind the curtain and saw the figure of a woman, allegedly Florence Cook, lying on the floor, her face covered with a red shawl. A number of other sitters were, at various times, allowed to see the same figure, but always the face was obscured. As Serjeant Cox commented:

"If the face was hidden under a shawl the proof fails entirely, for it is impossible for any of the persons present to say certainly that Miss Cook herself was lying there. All that is proved by this experiment is that while a form precisely resembling Miss Cook in face and figure was outside the curtain, a lady wearing her dress, or a dress like hers, was lying inside the curtain. But there is no proof whatever that it was Miss Cook's body. The concealment of the face by the shawl raises indeed a very strong presumption to the contrary.''

Equally unimpressed was another witness, J. Enmore Jones. His comment is particularly telling in that he was a convinced spiritualist. In an account published in *The Medium and Daybreak* he wrote:

"Last night the medium was in her bedroom, was unbound, and was entranced lying on the floor. The leader [Crookes] stood in front of the awning, and made himself very active every time that 'Katie' appeared; stooping down to, or with face almost touching the face of 'Katie'; physically, and unscientifically, hampering all her movements, so as in several instances to compel the spirit with her hand to knock the face away from her, though done in a playful manner; reminding me of a fussy mesmerizer, who suddenly finding himself in office, desires to show himself off to the audience. The results of the mannerisms of the awningkeeper, and the crowded state of the room, reduced the whole seance to principally that of 'Katie' showing herself at the awning, and busying herself with dividing bunches of flowers and giving to each visitor. I trust that at future seances the leader, whoever he may be, may not be a familiar half-showman and half-playactor, on more than respectful terms with the ghost; but let the spirit have 'sea-room,' for her own advantage and that of the visitors.

"I was much struck with the strong resemblance the spirit had to the medium last night, even to the color of the face; the mannerism of action also was the same, the voice was similar when joining with the sitters while singing in the bedroom behind the awning. To those who had not seen 'Katie' under other and test conditions the impression must have been that 'Katie' was Miss Cook, and Miss Cook 'Katie' in a state of undress."

This word-picture, Trevor Hall remarks, "would more appropriately describe the behaviour of a man whose judgment was temporarily impaired by a foolish infatuation than that of a scientist conducting a serious experiment." Jones's comment on the resemblance of "Katie" to Florence Cook called from Serjeant Cox the comment:

"When I saw them they were not merely resemblances; they were facsimiles. I had carefully noted the shape of the eyebrows, which cannot be altered, and they were the same in the medium and the form. The hands were identical. The movements of the body were precisely similar."

Not surprisingly, in view of the critical comment they were arousing, the series of seances was brought to a close, only one more following that attended by Enmore Jones. No independent persons were invited to this final sitting apart from Miss Florence Marryat, a completely unreliable witness whose glowing account of the seance was later disclaimed by Crookes with the comment, "There is not a word of truth in it." It is a measure of her extravagant and careless reporting that when her book containing the account, *There is No Death,* was published, *The Athenaeum* reviewed it under "Novels of the Week." An example of the flights of fantasy that Miss Marryat permitted herself is the statement in her book that Katie King frequently materialized in order to get into bed with Florence, whose husband, Miss Marryat claimed, had told her that he felt as if he had two wives and was never sure which was the earthly Florence.

Miss Marryat's testimony, as Hall points out, is important only because of its connection with the curious behaviour of Crookes, who recommended it to his readers in 1874 and declared at least some of it to be quite untrue in 1906. Most contributors to the literature of spiritualism, including Sir Arthur Conan Doyle, have chosen to ignore Crookes's disclaimer.

An important point to which Hall devotes considerable space is the strange reluctance of Crookes to answer the objections or meet the challenges of his critics, an attitude in marked contrast to the vigorous and vehement stand he had taken against those who sought to cast doubt on his reports concerning the investigation of D. D. Home. Even Conan Doyle, credulous and uncritical, made the comment:

"Without going to the length of subterfuge, he did unquestionably shirk the question. He refused to have his articles upon the subject republished, and he would not circulate the wonderful photographs in which the materialized Katie King stood arm-in-arm with himself. He was exceedingly cautious also in defining his position."

To many, these facts may seem damning enough. But independent substantiation is also forthcoming.

In 1959, it was disclosed that some time previously Mr. F. G. H. Anderson, a man of considerable education and intellectual attainment, had made statements to the Society for Psychical Research revealing that in 1893, when he was twenty-three years old, he had had an affair with Florence, who was then between thirty-five and forty, and whose husband was away from home. The affair began when he paid a visit to the Corners' home at Usk, and Florence, whom he described as "the most beautiful little thing—quite exceptional," made it quite clear from the beginning that she was willing to have an affair with him. He said:

"She was very highly sexed, and I can remember the scene of how it all started as if I saw it now. There was a large hall with a staircase leading upstairs and bending to form a sort of square as it ascended, so that one looked down on to the hall from above. In the drawing-room was a piano at which the daughter was practicing. Mrs. Corner told her she must practice well, and she would leave the door open so that she could verify that she was doing so.

"She came to me in the dining-room downstairs and said, 'I know what you want, I think,' and went upstairs. Shortly she leant over the banisters and called to me, 'Frankie, Frankie—come up.' I went up and she called me into her room and I found her very much undressed on the bed. And so it all began!"

During the course of the liaison, which continued for nearly a year, Florence told Anderson of her former relationship with Sir William Crookes, how she had been his mistress, having gone to Paris with him on several occasions and how she had practised her fraudulent mediumship. Anderson added:

"She used to keep a light burning at night in the bedroom, and told me that she did so because she had so often impersonated spirits and pretended these manifestations at seances that she became afraid that possibly there might have been such things, which might have a spite against her for her deceptions, and she had consequently a dislike of being in the dark.

"She told me that she had done all this in collusion with William Crookes (I am not sure whether he had at that time been knighted) and that she had been for some time his mistress; and that the materialization and assumption of earthly life by 'Katie King' (who was herself) was just a device by which she had been able to live in Crookes's house, under his wife's nose, without exciting too much suspicion. For the same reason, she said, she had been over to Paris with Crookes on several occasions."

Anderson thought that Crookes might have become sexually entangled with Florence before discovering she was a fraud, and by the time he did was much too involved either to expose her or break off the liaison. He also believed that Crookes "got money for Florence by means of the seances."

It is most significant that Anderson also alleged that Florrie had complained bitterly that her two sisters had, by means of fraudulent seances, persuaded a wealthy old man named Blackburn to leave money to them. It was during his intimacy with Florrie, said Anderson, that she used to describe the details of her sisters' frauds upon Blackburn.

Additional evidence also comes from quite another independent source, in the form of a statement made to Mrs. Eileen Garrett by M. H. A. Jules Bois, the French writer. M. Bois stated that as a very young man he too had an affair with Florence, who at the time was very much older than he. During the affair she had told him that the seances in 1874 were fraudulent and had been used by Crookes and herself to cover up their sexual liaison.

It is noteworthy that neither Anderson nor Bois made their statements with a view to personal publicity. On the contrary, Anderson wished his deposition to be kept as a confidential document by the SPR, and Bois was, as Hall says, "an elderly man and a Roman Catholic, whose conscience was disturbed lest he should die without revealing the information he possessed to a sympathetic psychical researcher."

In considering the mass of evidence which he has so painstakingly gathered and methodically set out, Hall suggests that a useful approach is firstly to try to decide, in isolation from her association with Crookes and her accounts to Anderson and Bois, whether Florence Cook was, in fact, a genuine medium. He points out that the many recorded instances of her exposure in flagrant trickery are, at the very least, extremely damaging. He also stressed the significance of the fact that another medium, Mary Showers—a friend of Florence with whom she once held a joint seance at Crookes's house, in which two alleged materializations walked arm-in-arm around his laboratory—was later detected in glaring imposture by Serjeant Cox. The conclusion here seems inescapable that either both were genuine or both fraudulent.

In the case of Kate, the younger sister of Florence, there is overwhelming evidence that she was nothing more than a calculating adventuress whose mediumship was wholly fraudulent. Like Florence, she was encouraged and assisted in its development by her mother, and the pair of them, says Hall, "seem to have devoted themselves from 1875 onwards to the unscrupulous extraction of large sums of money and property from Charles Blackburn, and they pursued their object with cruel and insatiable persistence until literally the day of his death." The fact that Florence, who must have been aware of their activities, remained on close and affectionate terms with them is a damning indication of her own character.

Furthermore, it must be remembered that Kate Cook began her career as a medium by stepping into the breach created when Florence fell out of favor with Blackburn. The development of her mediumship precisely duplicated that of her sister in a way suggesting that it was dependent on the same tricks. Here Hall comments:

"Living in the same house, Kate would be familiar with every detail of the various deceptions. All she needed was the guidance of Emma Cook [the mother], which was readily available, and the acquisition of the necessary skill and confidence which came with practice. She started, as Florence had done, by learning the simple trick of freeing herself from restraint (or even allowing the 'spirits' to tie a suitable slipknot as Florence did in her earliest days) and then standing on her chair in the Punch and Judy cabinet and producing 'spirit faces' at the aperture for the delighted spiritualists."

In view of our certain knowledge of Kate Cook's dishonesty, and the fact that both girls commenced their careers under the guidance and control of their mother, who was constantly in attendance at their early seances, Hall has good reason to ask, "Is it possible to believe that Emma Cook could have been both the reverent impresario in regard to genuine and incredible paranormal phenomena produced by Florence and, at the same time, the accomplice and mentor of the fraudulent Kate?"

There would seem to be little doubt also that not only Emma Cook, but Thomas Blyton, William Harrison and Edward Elgie Corner, all of whom profited substantially from the sisters' mediumistic activities, were well aware of their fraudulent nature; indeed, they were leading lights in the organization of the business as a money-making "racket."

If it is accepted that Florence Cook was fraudulent, then the conclusion that William Crookes was her accomplice—was himself a fraud—seems to follow inescapably. "His position as controller of the seances, his freedom to enter the cabinet and his own accounts of the conditions of the sittings make it clear beyond doubt that he was the one person who could not possibly have been deceived."

In the light of these facts, the statements of Anderson and Bois are clearly of the highest significance. She confessed to them that her mediumship was fraudulent, as was that of her sister. She even gave details of the methods of trickery employed, and further, revealed that they were used to extract large sums of money from Charles Blackburn, facts which Anderson and Bois could not conceivably have known from any other source. Her story that Crookes had been her lover and accomplice in fraud when he was ostensibly playing the part of a scientific investigator is also one that could not have been obtained, certainly in such details, except from the source alleged.

This, then, is the amazing story revealed in *The Spiritualists,* of one of the sorriest and most extraordinary swindles in "the whole sordid story of modern spiritualism."

Hall's book evoked much criticism, based mainly on the argument apparently accepted by Richet and the others mentioned above, that a scientist of Crookes's status would be incapable of dishonest behavior. In reply, Hall cites the many cases described in Vayson de Pradenne's treatise, *Les Fraudes en Archéologie Préhistorique* (Paris, 1932), and remarks that the melancholy stories of Glozel and Piltdown are too well known to merit more than a passing mention. He reminds us of the Thomas B. Wise scandal, which "demonstrated that the President of the Bibliographical Society was a proven forger, thief, and secret mutilator of rare books at the British Museum. Like Crookes, Wise's admirable contributions to our knowledge in his field were rewarded by high academic recognition. He was made an honorary M.A. of Oxford University and a Fellow of Worcester College." Hall also asks whether, "if confirmation is needed of the morass of folly and deceit into which a previously and distinguished married man of over forty can be drawn by sexual desire for a girl over twenty years younger than himself, need we look further than the affair of the British Minister for War and Christine Keeler?"⁹

REFERENCES

1. Iremonger, Lucille: *The Ghosts of Versailles.* London, 1957.
2. Salter, W. H.: "An Adventure," A note on the evidence, *Journ. SPR, 35*: 656:165-187.
3. Fourth Report of the Literary Committee: A theory of apparitions, Part 2, *Proc. SPR, 2*:180.
4. West, D. J.: The identity of "Jack the Ripper"; an examination of an alleged psychic solution, *Journ. SPR, 35*: 653:76-80.
5. Fournier d'Albe, E. E.: *The Life of Sir William Crookes.* London, 1923.
6. Collins, J. Abdy.: The whole case for survival, *Psychic News,* May 8, 1948.
7. Zorab, George: The Resurrection—a psychical analysis, *Tomorrow,* 2: 4:13-14.
8. Landau, Lucian: Psychical study as a background to Christian faith, *Light,* Autumn, 1959, pp. 173-184.
9. Hall, Trevor H.: Reply to Dr. Ian Stevenson's review of *The Spiritualists, Journ. ASPR, 58*: 1:57-65.

Chapter 12

THE POSITION TODAY—AND TOMORROW

> *"I didn't understand a word of it; but facts, or what*
> *a man believes to be facts, are always delightful.*
> *That mathematical fellow believed in his facts.*
> *So do I. Get your facts first, and"—the voice dies*
> *away to an almost inaudible drone—"then you can*
> *distort 'em as much as you please."*
>
> MARK TWAIN (reading an article on mathematics,
> as reported by Rudyard Kipling)

DURING the century or so since organized psychical research began, numerous attempts have been made to explain the phenomena of psi and to fit them into our existing concepts of the scheme of things. To do so must be the long-term aim of all parapsychologists, and when psi phenomena are regarded as "normal" rather than "paranormal" we shall recognize that this aim has indeed been achieved.

In my view, however, it is open to serious question whether the time has come when such theorizing can be of great value. We are, at present, very much at the stage of describing rather than explaining, and much of this describing can still only be in terms of "what it is not." Thus, for instance, it is generally accepted that telepathy cannot be some form of "mental radio," because telepathy seems to operate quite independently of the distance separating the persons concerned, whereas electro-magnetic radiations conform to the inverse square law.

In my submission, therefore, at present the first task of the parapsychologist is to get his facts—and get them straight. To do this obviously calls for a fair knowledge of physical science, for clearly, a reasonable understanding of *normal* phenomena is a prerequisite for the consideration of the paranormal. This does not mean, of course, that all students of the subject need to be learned physicists, qualified chemists, and expert statisticians; the Renaissance ideal of the polymath, learned in all fields of study, has long been unattainable in a world of increasing complexity and consequent specialization. Unless, however, an investigator has a broad idea of the scope and achievements of modern scientific technology, and takes them fully into consideration, any attempt to carry out psychical research is virtually futile.

In the absence of detailed knowledge of a specific subject, the important thing is to recognize when such specialized knowledge is needed and to be able to call upon someone who possesses it. This, nowadays, is one of the most valuable of the purposes served by the SPR and similar bodies—specialists of all kinds are members and their aid can be enlisted in any problem that seems to be connected with their particular field of specialization.

As in all scientific investigation, a working hypothesis that springs from the facts—all the facts—already available may often suggest a fruitful line of experiment. I think, however, it is true to say that every theory so far advanced as a comprehensive explanation of psi has been shown inadequate to fit the known facts—and it seems that all the theorists have made the same error, of trying to build theories upon insufficient facts. Charles Darwin liked to "begin with a good body of facts and not from principle, in which I always suspect some fallacy." Podmore too preferred this approach; and though we may have learned a little more since his time we still do not know nearly enough for theories.

It is equally true that any theory of psychology must be inadequate if it fails to take into account paranormal phenomena, whatever their explanation, and whether or not they are attributable to some extra-physical aspect of man. Indeed, it becomes impossible to regard psychology and parapsychology as two distinct subjects. Dr. Rhine states: "The prefix *para* added to psychology serves well enough the purpose of marking off a section of the general field of psychology for such time as the distinction is needed." But unless orthodox psychologists broaden their outlook it may well be that the parapsychology of today proves the forerunner of the psychology of tomorrow.

Psychical research, for so long mistrusted by the scientist, feared by the theologian, and scorned by the man in the street, all of whom, in general, dismissed it as "dabbling in the occult," seems at last, as parapsychology, to be achieving a measure of respectability. Its complete acceptance will inevitably be slow, but it can best be achieved by psychical researchers insisting on maintaining the highest and most rigorous standards. The comment of James Harvey Robinson in *The Humanizing of Knowledge* applies in many fields, but in none more appositely than parapsychology.

"Of all human ambitions an open mind eagerly expectant of new discoveries and ready to remold convictions in the light of added knowledge and dispelled ignorance and misapprehensions, is the noblest, the rarest, and the most difficult to achieve."

INDEX

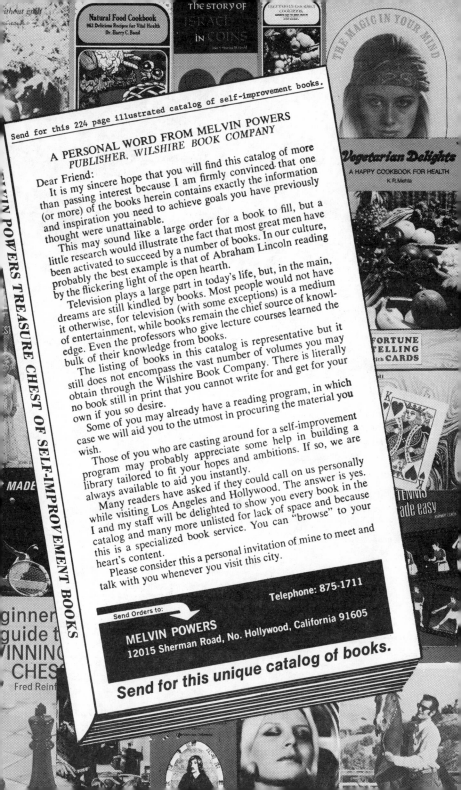

Melvin Powers
SELF-IMPROVEMENT
LIBRARY

ABILITY TO LOVE *Dr. Allan Fromme*	$2.00
ACT YOUR WAY TO SUCCESSFUL LIVING *Neil & Margaret Rau*	2.00
ADVANCED TECHNIQUES OF HYPNOSIS *Melvin Powers*	1.00
ANIMAL HYPNOSIS *Dr. F. A. Völgyesi*	2.00
ASTROLOGY: A FASCINATING HISTORY *P. Naylor*	2.00
ASTROLOGY: HOW TO CHART YOUR HOROSCOPE *Max Heindel*	2.00
ASTROLOGY: YOUR PERSONAL SUN-SIGN GUIDE *Beatrice Ryder*	2.00
ASTROLOGY FOR EVERYDAY LIVING *Janet Harris*	2.00
ASTROLOGY GUIDE TO GOOD HEALTH *Alexandra Kayhle*	2.00
ASTROLOGY MADE EASY *Astarte*	2.00
ASTROLOGY MADE PRACTICAL *Alexandra Kayhle*	2.00
ASTROLOGY, ROMANCE, YOU AND THE STARS *Anthony Novell*	2.00
BEGINNER'S GUIDE TO WINNING CHESS *Fred Reinfeld*	2.00
BETTER CHESS — How to Play *Fred Reinfeld*	2.00
BICYCLING FOR FUN AND GOOD HEALTH *Kenneth E. Luther*	2.00
BOOK OF TALISMANS, AMULETS & ZODIACAL GEMS *William Pavitt*	3.00
BRIDGE BIDDING MADE EASY *Edwin Kantar*	5.00
BRIDGE CONVENTIONS *Edwin Kantar*	4.00
CHECKERS MADE EASY *Tom Wiswell*	2.00
CHESS IN TEN EASY LESSONS *Larry Evans*	2.00
CHESS MADE EASY *Milton L. Hanauer*	2.00
CHESS MASTERY — A New Approach *Fred Reinfeld*	2.00
CHESS PROBLEMS FOR BEGINNERS *edited by Fred Reinfeld*	2.00
CHESS SECRETS REVEALED *Fred Reinfeld*	2.00
CHESS STRATEGY — An Expert's Guide *Fred Reinfeld*	2.00
CHESS TACTICS FOR BEGINNERS *edited by Fred Reinfeld*	2.00
CHESS THEORY & PRACTICE *Morry & Mitchell*	2.00
CHILDBIRTH WITH HYPNOSIS *William S. Kroger, M.D.*	2.00
COIN COLLECTING FOR BEGINNERS *Burton Hobson & Fred Reinfeld*	2.00
CONCENTRATION—A Guide to Mental Mastery *Mouni Sadhu*	2.00
CONVERSATION MADE EASY *Elliot Russell*	1.00
CULPEPER'S HERBAL REMEDIES *Dr. Nicholas Culpeper*	2.00
CYBERNETICS WITHIN US *Y. Saparina*	3.00
DOCTOR PSYCHO-CYBERNETICS *Maxwell Maltz, M.D.*	2.50
DOG TRAINING MADE EASY & FUN *John W. Kellogg*	2.00
DREAMS & OMENS REVEALED *Fred Gettings*	2.00
DR. LINDNER'S SPECIAL WEIGHT CONTROL METHOD	1.00
DYNAMIC THINKING *Melvin Powers*	1.00
ENCYCLOPEDIA OF MODERN SEX & LOVE TECHNIQUES *R. Macandrew*	2.00
EXAM SECRET *Dennis B. Jackson*	1.00
EXTRASENSORY PERCEPTION *Simeon Edmunds*	2.00
FAST GOURMET COOKBOOK *Poppy Cannon*	2.50
FORTUNE TELLING WITH CARDS *P. Foli*	2.00
GAYELORD HAUSER'S NEW GUIDE TO INTELLIGENT REDUCING	3.00
GOULD'S GOLD & SILVER GUIDE TO COINS *Maurice Gould*	2.00
GREATEST POWER IN THE UNIVERSE *U. S. Andersen*	4.00

Melvin Powers
SELF-IMPROVEMENT
LIBRARY

Melvin Powers
SELF-IMPROVEMENT
LIBRARY

WILSHIRE HORSE LOVERS' LIBRARY

AMATEUR HORSE BREEDER *A. C. Leighton Hardman*	2.00
AMERICAN QUARTER HORSE IN PICTURES *Margaret Cabell Self*	2.00
APPALOOSA HORSE *Bill & Dona Richardson*	2.00
ARABIAN HORSE *Reginald S. Summerhays*	2.00
AT THE HORSE SHOW *Margaret Cabell Self*	2.00
BACK-YARD FOAL *Peggy Jett Pittinger*	2.00
BACK-YARD HORSE *Peggy Jett Pittinger*	2.00
BASIC DRESSAGE *Jean Froissard*	2.00
BITS—THEIR HISTORY, USE AND MISUSE *Louis Taylor*	2.00
CAVALRY MANUAL OF HORSEMANSHIP *Gordon Wright*	2.00
COMPLETE TRAINING OF HORSE AND RIDER *Colonel Alois Podhajsky*	3.00
DRESSAGE—A study of the Finer Points in Riding *Henry Wynmalen*	2.00
DRIVING HORSES *Sallie Walrond*	2.00
EQUITATION *Jean Froissard*	3.00
FIRST AID FOR HORSES *Dr. Charles H. Denning, Jr.*	2.00
FUN OF RAISING A COLT *Rubye & Frank Griffith*	2.00
FUN ON HORSEBACK *Margaret Cabell Self*	2.00
HORSE OWNER'S CONCISE GUIDE *Elsie V. Hanauer*	2.00
HORSE SELECTION & CARE FOR BEGINNERS *George H. Conn*	2.00
HORSE SENSE—A complete guide to riding and care *Alan Deacon*	4.00
HORSEBACK RIDING FOR BEGINNERS *Louis Taylor*	3.00
HORSEBACK RIDING MADE EASY & FUN *Sue Henderson Coen*	2.00
HORSES—Their Selection, Care & Handling *Margaret Cabell Self*	2.00
ILLUSTRATED HORSE MANAGEMENT—400 Illustrations *Dr. E. Mayhew*	5.00
ILLUSTRATED HORSEBACK RIDING FOR BEGINNERS *Jeanne Mellin*	2.00
JUMPING—Learning and Teaching *Jean Froissard*	2.00
LIPIZZANERS AND THE SPANISH RIDING SCHOOL *W. Reuter*	2.00
MORGAN HORSE IN PICTURES *Margaret Cabell Self*	2.00
POLICE HORSES *Judith Campbell*	2.00
PROBLEM HORSES *Reginald S. Summerhays* Tested Guide for Curing Most Common & Serious Horse Behavior Habits	2.00
RESCHOOLING THE THOROUGHBRED *Peggy Jett Pittenger*	2.00
SCHOOLING YOUR YOUNG HORSE *George Wheatley*	2.00
TEACHING YOUR HORSE TO JUMP *W. J. Froud*	2.00
THE LAW AND YOUR HORSE *Edward H. Greene*	3.00
TRAIL HORSES & TRAIL RIDING *Anne & Perry Westbrook*	2.00
TREATING HORSE AILMENTS *G. W. Serth*	2.00
WONDERFUL WORLD OF PONIES *Peggy Jett Pittinger*	4.00
YOUR PONY BOOK *Hermann Wiederhold*	2.00
YOUR WESTERN HORSE *Nelson C. Nye*	2.00

Books of Special Interest

DOG TRAINING MADE EASY & FUN *John W. Kellogg*	2.00
PIGEONS: HOW TO RAISE AND TRAIN THEM *William H. Allen, Jr.*	2.00

The books listed above can be obtained from your book dealer or directly from Wilshire Book Company. When ordering, please remit 10c per book postage. Send for our free 224 page illustrated catalog of self-improvement books.

Wilshire Book Company
12015 Sherman Road, No. Hollywood, California 91605

Notes

Notes

Notes